DRAW PEOPLE

Benedict Rubbra

DRAW PEOPLE

Edited by David and Brenda Herbert

ADAM & CHARLES BLACK · LONDON

*Draw People** first published 1984
by A & C Black (Publishers) Ltd
35 Bedford Row, London WC1R 4JH

© 1984 A & C Black (Publishers) Ltd

*This volume contains material already
published in
Draw the Human Body © A & C Black (Publishers) Ltd 1981
Draw Faces and Expressions © A & C Black (Publishers) Ltd 1982
Draw Children © A & C Black (Publishers) Ltd 1981
Draw Portraits © Pitman House Ltd 1980

Draw people.
  1. Figure drawing   2. Human figure in art
  I. Herbert, David, *1927–*   2. Herbert, Brenda
743′.4   NC765

  ISBN 0–7136–2619–4
  ISBN 0–7136–2618–6 Pbk

ISBN 0-7136-2619-4
ISBN 0-7136-2618-6   Pbk

Printed in Great Britain
by BAS Printers Limited, Over Wallop, Hampshire

Contents

Introduction

Making a start

Learning to draw is largely a matter of practice and observation—so draw as much and as often as you can, and use your eyes all the time.

Look around you—at chairs, tables, plants, people, pets, building, your hand holding this book. Everything is worth drawing. The time spent on a drawing is not important. It is the intensity and purpose with which it is done that matters.

Carry a sketchbook with you whenever possible, and don't be shy of using it in public, either for quick notes to be used later or for a finished drawing.

Roy Spencer

To do an interesting drawing, you must enjoy it. Even if you start on something that doesn't particularly interest you, you will probably find that the act of drawing it—and looking at it in a new way—creates its own excitement. The less you think about how you are drawing and the more you think about what you are drawing, the better your drawing will be.

Be as bold as you dare. It's your piece of paper and you can do what you like with it. Experiment with the biggest piece of paper and the boldest, softest piece of chalk or crayon you can find, filling the paper with lines— scribbles, lettering, anything—to get a feeling of freedom. Even if you think you have a gift for tiny delicate line drawings with a fine pen or pencil, this is worth trying. It will give you an idea of how vivid a drawing can be.

Be self-critical. The aim is to get the drawing right; so alter it to make it so using an eraser as little as possible. This does not mean retracing lines more heavily. A drawing is the sum total of all your efforts to get it right. Neatness does not make a good drawing.

It is preferable to draw in black and white, and to use colour when it says something about the subject which you cannot say in black and white alone.

You can learn a certain amount from copying other people's drawings. But you will learn more from a drawing done from direct observation of the subject or even out of your head, however still and unsatisfactory the results may seem at first.

A lot can be learned by practice and from books, but a teacher can be a great help. If you get the chance, don't hesitate to join a class—even one evening a week can do a lot of good.

John Raynes

What to draw with

John Raynes

Pencils are graded according to hardness, from 6H (the hardest) through 5H, 4H, 3H, 2H to H; then HB; then B, through 1B, 2B, 3B, 4B, 5B up to 6B (the softest). For most purposes, a soft pencil (HB or softer) is best. If you keep it sharp, it will draw as fine a line as a hard pencil but with less pressure, which makes it easier to control.

Charcoal, which is very soft, is by nature useful for bold drawing, but with skill you can achieve great subtlety with it. Charcoal pencils, such as the Royal Sovereign, are also very useful.

Wax crayons (also soft) are not easily smudged or erased. You can scrape a line away from a drawing on good quality paper, or partly scrape a drawing to get special effects.

Conté crayons, wood-cased or in solid sticks, are available in various degrees of hardness, and in several colours. The cased crayons are easy to sharpen, but the solid sticks are more fun—you can use the side of the stick for large areas of tone. Conté is harder than charcoal, but it is also easy to smudge. The black is very intense.

Pastels are very soft and available in a wide range of colours, though these may be limited in use. They need to be spray-fixed.

Pens vary as much as pencils or crayons. The Gillott 659 is a very popular crowquill pen. Ink has a quality of its own, but of course it cannot be erased. Mapping pens are only suitable for delicate detail and minute cross-hatching.

Roy Spencer

Special artists' pens such as the Gillott 303 or Gillott 404 allow you a more varied line, according to the angle at which you hold them and the pressure you use.

Reed, bamboo and quill pens are good for bold lines. You can make the nib end narrower or wider with the help of a sharp knife or razor blade. This kind of pen has to be dipped frequently into the ink.

Fountain pens are convenient for sketching, provided they make a fairly even line in any direction. Rapidograph and Rotring pens are not generally desirable. They are really for mechanical drawing.

Inks vary according to the manufacturer. Waterproof Indian ink is generally the most useful. If it is too thick and clogs the pen, water it down with distilled water or boiled water out of the kettle. It is very necessary to use a waterproof ink if you intend to combine line and wash.

Ball point pens make a drawing look a bit mechanical, but they are cheap and fool-proof and useful for quick notes and scribbles.

Fibre pens are only slightly better, and their points tend to wear down quickly.

Felt pens are useful for quick notes and sketches, but are not good for more elaborate and finished drawings.

Brushes are most versatile drawing instruments and therefore very difficult to use. The Chinese and Japanese until recently have never used anything else, even for writing. The biggest sable brush has a fine point, and the smallest brush laid on its side provides a line broader than the broadest nib. Sables are very expensive but you can find cheaper brushes which are less springy and good to use.

A wash of watercolour or ink may be used to extend a pen or pencil drawing. It should not be used for effect but to say something about the subject, such as the pattern of colour or the light and shade.

John Raynes

Roy Spencer

9

What to draw on

'What to draw on' and 'what to draw with' depend on each other. A pencil drawing needs fairly smooth paper with a good 'bite'—the smaller the drawing, the smoother the paper. A pen drawing needs a hard, white paper; and a pen-and-wash drawing a softer, more absorbent paper. Try out as many different surfaces as possible.

Ordinary, inexpensive paper is often as good as anything else: for example, brown and buff wrapping paper (Kraft paper) and lining for wallpaper have surfaces which are particularly suitable for charcoal and soft crayons. Some writing and duplicating papers are best for pen drawings. But there are many papers and brands made specially for the artist.

Bristol board is a smooth, hard white board designed for fine pen work.

Ledger Bond paper ('cartridge' in the UK), the most usual drawing paper, is available in a variety of surfaces—smooth, 'not surface' (semi-rough), rough.

Watercolour papers also come in various grades of smoothness. They are thick, high-quality papers, expensive but pleasant to use.

Ingres paper is mainly for pastel drawings. It has a soft, furry surface and is made in many light colours—grey, pink, blue, buff, etc.

Sketchbooks made up from nearly all these papers are available. Choose one with thin, smooth paper to begin with. Thin paper means more pages, and a smooth surface is best to record detail.

Lay-out pads make useful sketchbooks. Although their covers are not stiff, you can easily insert a stiff piece of card to act as firm backing to your drawing. The paper is semi-transparent, but this can be useful—almost as tracing paper—if you want to make a new, different version of your last drawing.

An improvised sketchbook can be just as good as a bought one—or better. Find two pieces of thick card, sandwich a stack of paper, which may be of different kinds, between them and clip together at either end.

Pen on very smooth cartridge

Pen on ordinary cartridge

Roy Spencer

Willow charcoal on watercolour paper (not surface)

John Raynes

11

Perspective: general

You can be an artist without knowing anything about perspective. Five hundred years ago, when some of the great masterpieces of all time were painted, the word did not even exist. But most beginners want to know something about it in order to make their drawings appear three-dimensional rather than flat, so here is a short guide.

The further away an object is, the smaller it looks.

All parallel horizontal lines that are directly opposite you, at right-angles to your line of vision, remain parallel.

All horizontal lines that are in fact parallel but go away from you will appear to converge at eye-level at the same vanishing point on the horizon. Lines that are above your eye-level will seem to run downwards towards the vanishing point; lines that are below your eye-level will run upwards. You can check the angles of these lines against a pencil held horizontally at eye-level.

The larger and closer any object is, the bigger the front of it will seem to be in relation to the part furthest away, or to any other more distant object. Its actual shape will appear foreshortened or distorted. A matchbox close to you will appear larger and more distorted than a distant house, and if you are drawing a building seen at an angle through a window, the window frame will be larger and more distorted than the building.

If the side of an object is facing you, one vanishing point is enough; but if the corner is facing you, two vanishing points will be needed.

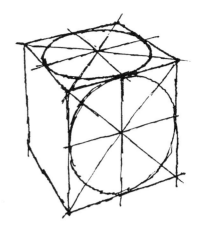

Diagonal lines drawn between the opposite angles of a square or rectangle will meet at a point which is half-way along its length or breadth. This remains true when the square or rectangle is foreshortened. You may find it helpful to remember this when you are drawing surfaces with equal divisions—for example, a tiled floor or the divisions between window panes—or deciding where to place the point of a roof or the position of windows on a facade.

When drawing a circular shape, the following is useful: a square drawn round a circle will touch the circle at the centre point of each of its sides. A foreshortened circle will turn into an elipse, but will still touch the centre points of each side of a similarly foreshortened square. However distored the square, the circle will remain a true elipse but will seem to tilt as the square moves to left or right of the vanishing point. The same is true of half circles.

You may tend to exaggerate the apparent depth of top surfaces because you know they are square or rectangular and want to show this in your drawing.

You can check the correct apparent depth of any receding plane by using a pencil or ruler held at eye-level and measuring the proportions on it with your thumb. If you use a ruler you can actually read off the various proportions.

Check the position of parts of a drawing against a horizontal or vertical. We are all agreed as to what they are.

The same applies when you are drawing people. If, for example, you try to draw a foreshortened forehead or arm you will tend to draw it the shape you know it to be rather than the shape it appears to be from your viewpoint. Again, measuring one proportion against another will help you to make your drawing look right.

Although perspective comes close to what we see, it is nevertheless a system of drawing and only makes sense when the view is seen within limited angles of vision.

Roy Spencer

Perspective: people

All objects on your eye-level, whether they are close to you or far away, and (if they are people) whether standing or sitting, must always be on the same horizontal in your picture.

Make perspective studies from real life scenes. Draw a line across your paper to represent your eye level. Then (without worrying about the quality of your drawing) plot the positions of the heads and feet of the people in the scene in front of you. Discover the point at which parallel horizontal lines converge. The diagrammatic sketches here show the process gone through to produce the drawing on the right.

Roy Spencer

Roy Spencer

The eye-level need not of course be that of figures in the scene. You may
be sitting down or at a higher level. If you are seated, the nearer the standing
figures the higher their heads will be. Try some perspective studies with
different eye-levels and draw from a subject to see how these principles are
borne out in reality.

The Human Body

Roy Spencer

In general

The idea of a drawing comes from observation; its execution comes from experience, and this can be greatly helped by your choice of materials. Always use those materials which make the techniques as easy as possible, and once you have chosen these, don't change to others if a particular drawing is not going well. The fault probably doesn't lie with the materials.

Drawings of the nude, as of any other subject, can take many different forms. They can be linear or tonal, very descriptive or almost abstract, large or small, detailed or broadly sketched, etc. Try various kinds. Compare the examples on these two pages.

Start your nude drawing with the head; it is the most familiar part of a figure and is therefore the most suitable part to establish first—as something 'fixed' against which you can measure and relate the rest of the drawing.

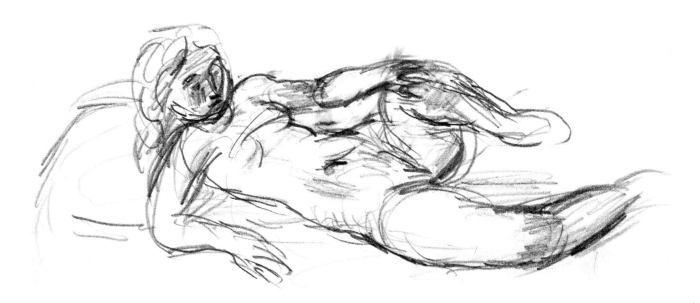

The human figure is the most interesting single object there is, and has been used as a motif in art throughout history. It has great expressive power and offers an extraordinary variety of forms.

The figure should be used, particularly at first, as a subject of study and to help your drawing generally; not as an attempt to produce works of art.

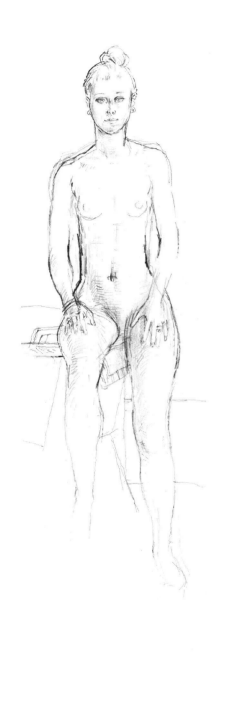

In this drawing, the head was the starting point. Try to establish the features as accurately as possible. The separate drawing on the right may help in understanding the head. Judge the angle it leans from the horizontal and make the eyes and mouth belong to the front plane. Treat the top and side as planes at right-angles to this front plane. The whole must be a complete solid rather than just a mask. Hold your pencil at arm's length towards the model, and measure the distance from the chin to the nipple, comparing it with the size of the head. The nipple is vertically below the left eye, and the same vertical runs through the tip of the fingers of the left hand. By careful observation you can discover other relationships which will help you to fix the position of other parts. The right hand is an example, but try to make it seem nearer to you than the shoulder. It is important to draw the arm of the sofa, because it both supports the figure and justifies the position of the figure's right hand and arm.

With a sitting or standing figure, the head is the highest part, so you can draw down the figure without your hand covering up what you have just done. Although the relationship between one part of the drawing to another is very important, the beginner will generally find it easier to start by drawing one part almost completely. In any case, don't sketch in the whole drawing first, since the result is bound to be entirely inaccurate and therefore no help at all. If you have any choice over where you draw from, a three-quarter view is easier than one from front or side.

These drawings of different views of the same pose show that the problems are more exposed in a view which is less frontal. In a frontal view the parts that make up the figure are more easily identified, and the drawing looks like the subject long before the forms are really drawn.

A figure needs a setting, however simple, or it will appear to float aimlessly in the middle of your sheet of paper. If you relate it to its surroundings, you will give it a sense of time and place. You will also find the proportions easier to establish. You can learn a lot from making drawings that concentrate on background, omitting almost all detail from the figure.

The nude in perspective

Much advice usually given on perspective suggests how you can convey the illusion of distance and three dimensions through the *lines* of your drawing. It is easier to think in terms of diminishing *planes*. If you try to represent the main *surfaces* of the figure with a feeling of direction and position in space, an impression of space will quickly emerge on the paper— and this is what perspective is about. Think of a cube and of how you would convey its three planes on paper, and try to see how this principle can be applied to your drawing of figures.

Once a sense of space is created on your paper by perspective (see right), any number of figures may be put in.

The figure here shows two planes at right-angles to each other—a front and a side plane. The raised position of the model forced me to convey this aspect of perspective. The sketch on the right is over-pedantic but elaborates the idea of the surfaces in perspective.

The distance between you and the model will greatly affect your view. The nearer you are, the steeper and more vital will be the perspective, since the subject will appear more solid and real.

Of the two drawings below, the first was made about twenty feet from the model, and the second about half that distance.

The drawing opposite was made very close to the model. Notice how steeply you look down onto the legs and feet.

Measuring

A plumb-line, held in front of you, will discover what parts of the body are on the same vertical as each other. But it is easier to discover a vertical than to judge an angle. With the figure on this page, you can find the position of each feature by first drawing a vertical line downwards through the left eye.

Against a ruler held at arm's length you can, for example, measure the distance from eye to chin to collarbone etc. Then you can measure distances to right and left of this 'centre' line and so make an accurate drawing of the whole figure.

Notice that your eye level is at the model's waist; you look up at the head and down at the feet. The torso and leg on the right of the drawing have approximately their natural length; whereas, on the other side, the length from shoulder to leg is shorter because the figure is slightly tilted.

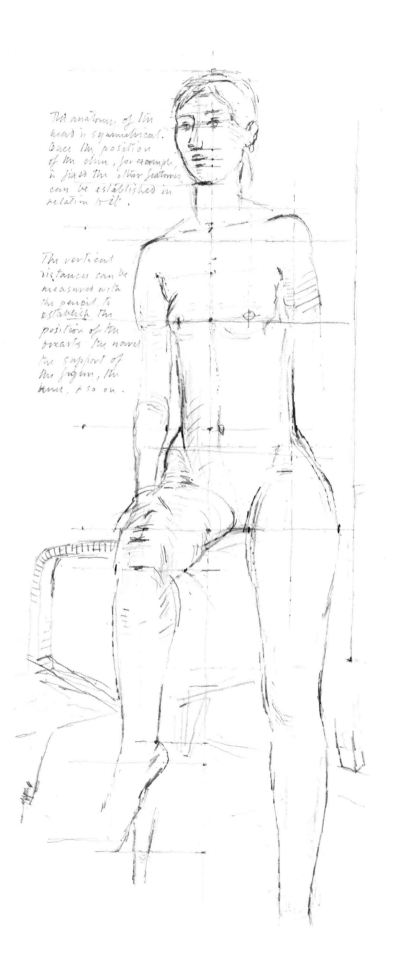

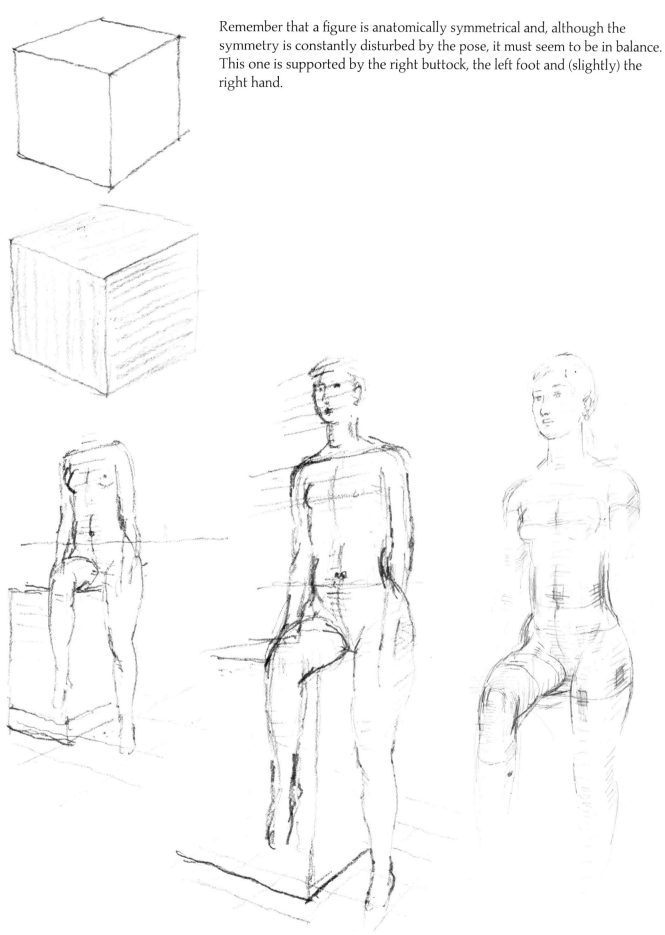

Remember that a figure is anatomically symmetrical and, although the symmetry is constantly disturbed by the pose, it must seem to be in balance. This one is supported by the right buttock, the left foot and (slightly) the right hand.

Anatomy: general articulation

If you take something from a high shelf, bend down and put it on the floor, you will appreciate the amazing articulation of the human body. A general understanding of articulation is more valuable than a detailed knowledge of bones and muscles; but both are worthwhile, provided you realise that anatomical knowledge is no substitute for observation. It is useful merely because it helps to interpret what you see.

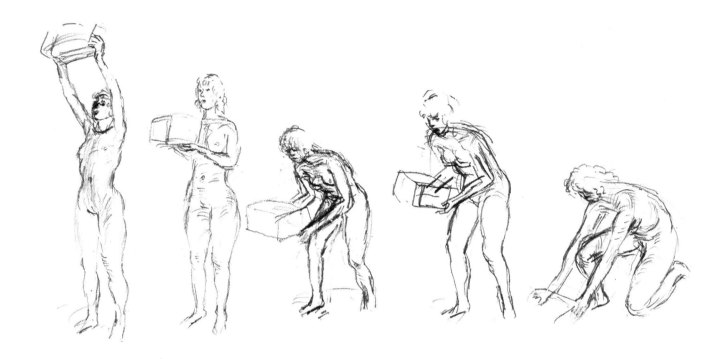

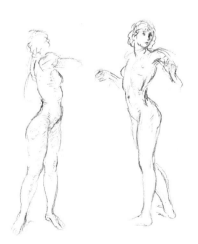

Throughout this book, I have not distinguished between the male and female figure—using female models almost always because, for psychological reasons, there have always been more nude females than males in art. The differences in a male and a female skeleton are small, the female's being lighter, her shoulders narrower and the angle and proportion of her pelvis different. The muscles are the same but differently developed—as indeed they are in people of the same sex. It is mostly the outer covering that distinguishes the sexes, and usually the female anatomy is more concealed by a layer of fat.

Those parts of the skeleton that are near the surface need attention (see the three skeletons here), and it is helpful to understand the character of various joints. The whole of the spine is usually visible, but it is particularly noticeable just above the shoulders and where it joins the pelvis. The collarbones are always visible, and so too are the shoulder blades (back view) and lower ribs (front view) particularly when arms or shoulders are raised. The crests of the pelvis can be seen on either side of the stomach, and the head of the femur on a level with the pubis (the joint itself is further in). The bones at elbow, wrist, knee and ankle are always visible.

The drawings below show that knowledge of the lengths of various bones can help to get proportions right.

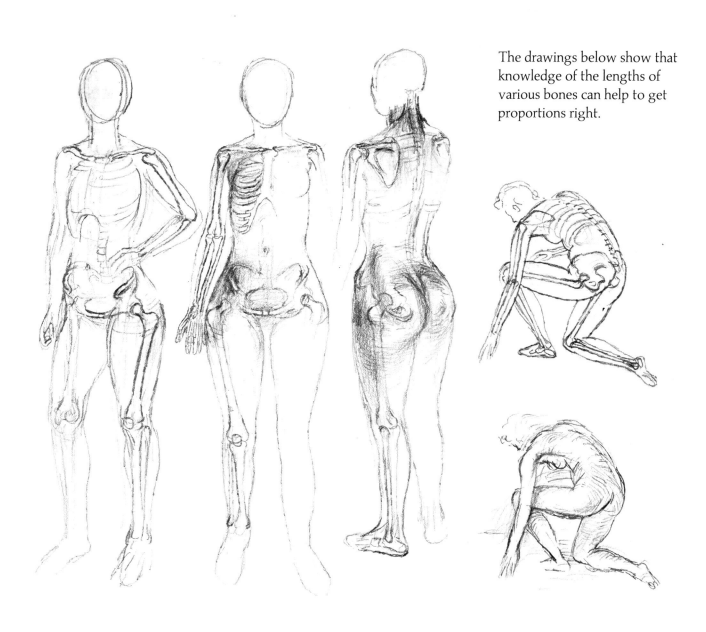

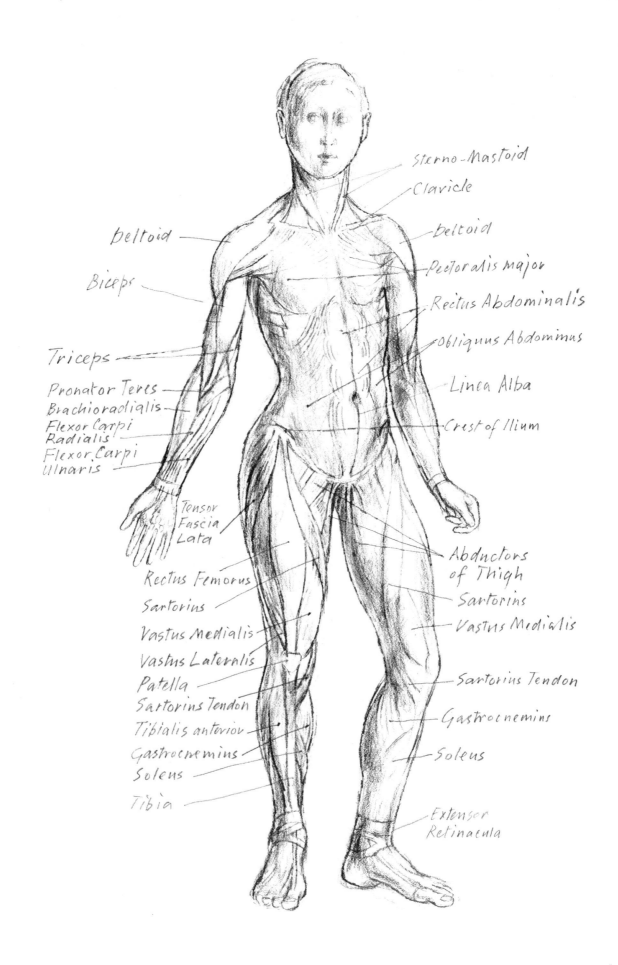

Sterno-Mastoid

Clavicle

Deltoid

Deltoid

Pectoralis major

Biceps

Rectus Abdominalis

obliquus Abdominus

Triceps

Linea Alba

Pronator Teres

Brachioradialis

Crest of Ilium

Flexor Carpi
Radialis

Flexor Carpi
Ulnaris

Tensor
Fascia
Lata

Abductors
of Thigh

Rectus Femorus

Sartorius

Sartorius

Vastus Medialis

Vastus Medialis

Vastus Laternlis

Patella

Sartorius Tendon

Sartorius Tendon

Gastrocnemins

Tibialis anterior

Gastrocnemins

Soleus

Soleus

Tibia

Extensor
Retinacula

32

Anatomy: detail

These two drawings show the main surface features of the human anatomy—in considerable detail—in a way that many artists of the past found essential to their work. Some knowledge of the larger anatomical forms can help to understand the figure in a particular pose—and can help too when you are drawing people when they are not nude. But remember the information is an aid to observation, not an aim in itself.

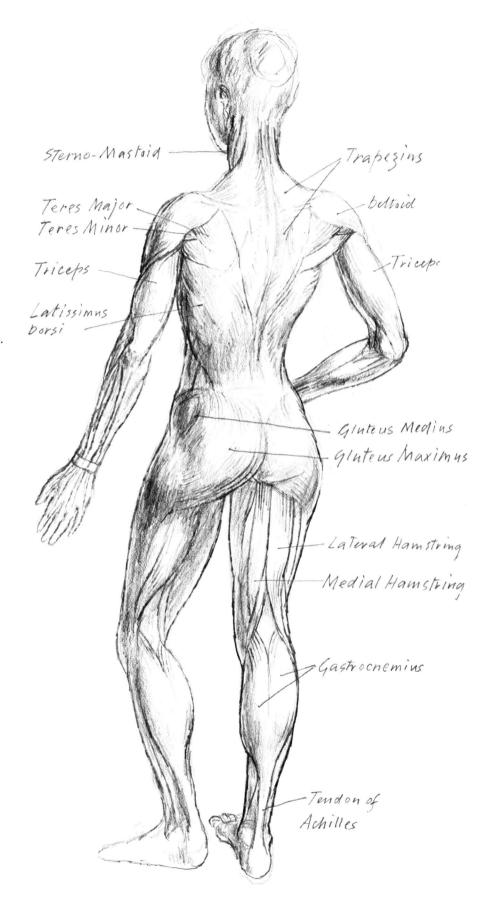

Sterno-Mastoid

Teres Major
Teres Minor

Triceps

Latissimus Dorsi

Trapezius

Deltoid

Triceps

Gluteus Medius
Gluteus Maximus

Lateral Hamstring

Medial Hamstring

Gastrocnemius

Tendon of Achilles

Standing

Get your model to stand symmetrically with his or her weight evenly distributed on both feet. Hold a plum line in front of the centre of the figure. Now get the model to move the weight from one foot to another, turn the body etc without moving the feet. Against the plumb line, you will see how the position of the head and every other part changes, as the figure adjusts to keep the whole body in balance. Note also how the tensions in the anatomy change. Extend this exercise to make drawings of many poses with the position of the feet unchanged.

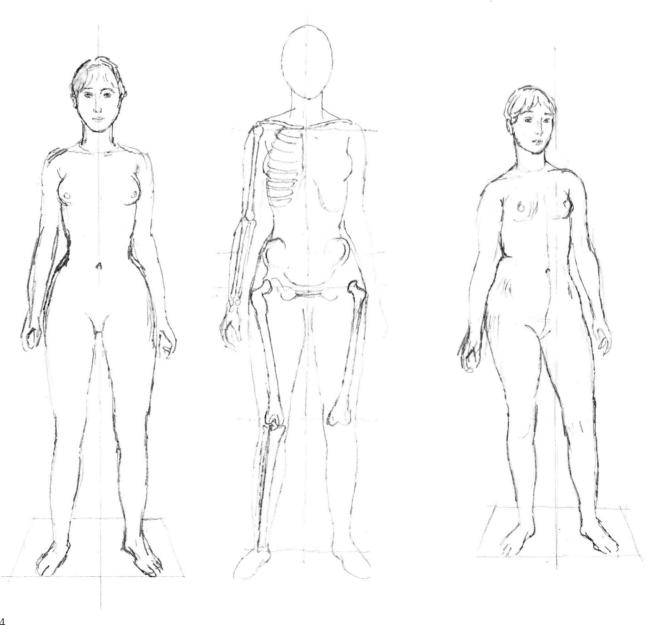

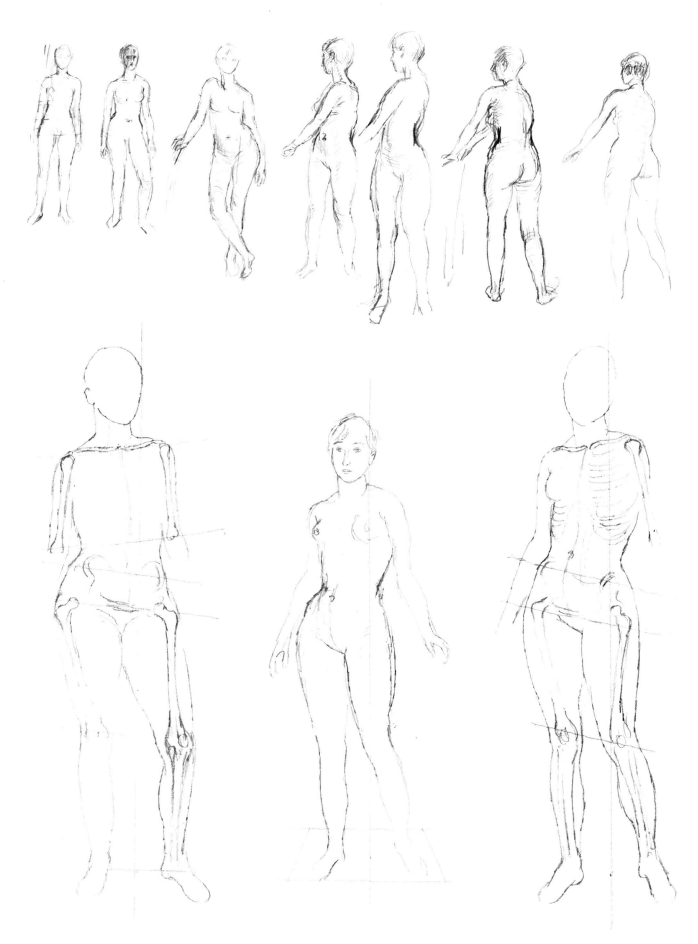

Make comparative drawings of the same pose from different angles.

Then try a standing pose in which the figure is partly supported by a hand and notice how the balance of the figure is altered. It is important to observe which parts of the body are supporting or in tension, and which are relaxed and giving way to gravity.

Drawing is understanding as well as seeing. It should be more than merely copying what you see before you. Your observation must be intense and purposeful always, and what you put on paper as a result must be equally purposeful.

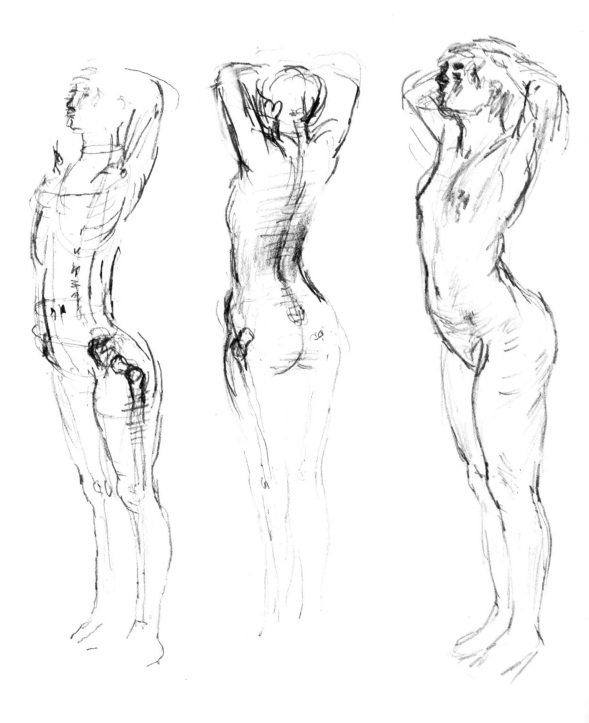

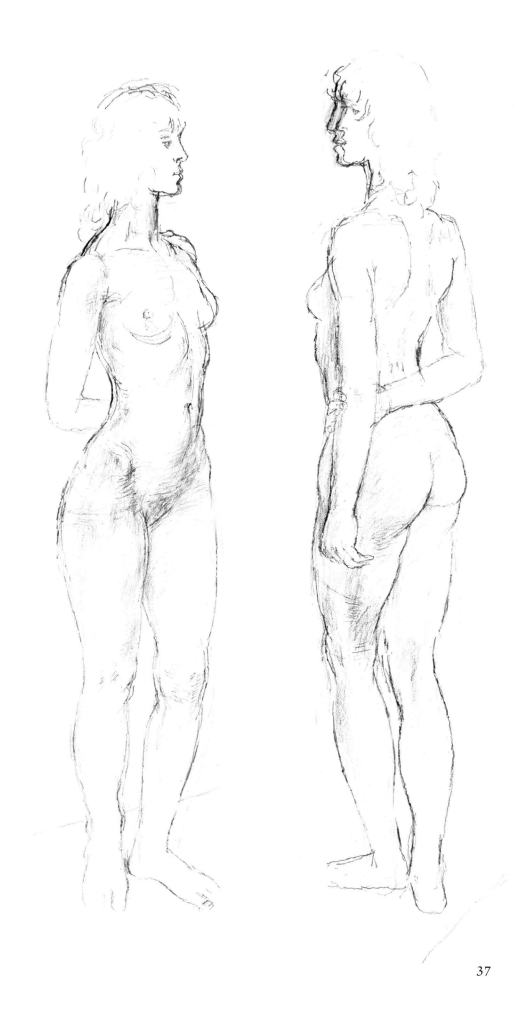

The shoulder

Anatomically the shoulder is complex. It can move up and down, forwards and backwards; and the arm can move in a complete circle—which is very different from the limited movement the leg can make from the hip. The shoulder's only fixed connection is through the collarbone, which is joined by cartilage to the breast bone. Examine a skeleton if you can or explore your own shoulder to see how it works. Using a model, draw the shoulder with the arm in various positions, as I have opposite.

In back views you will find the scapula fairly easily. Notice its mobility, its position varying with the position of the arm.

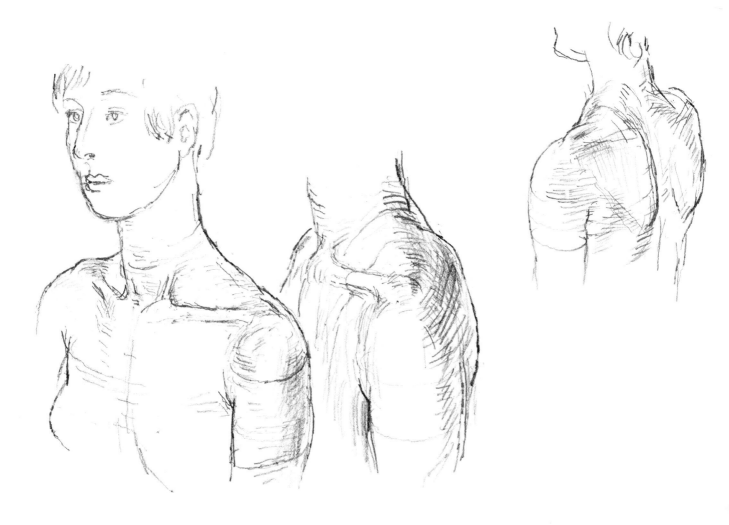

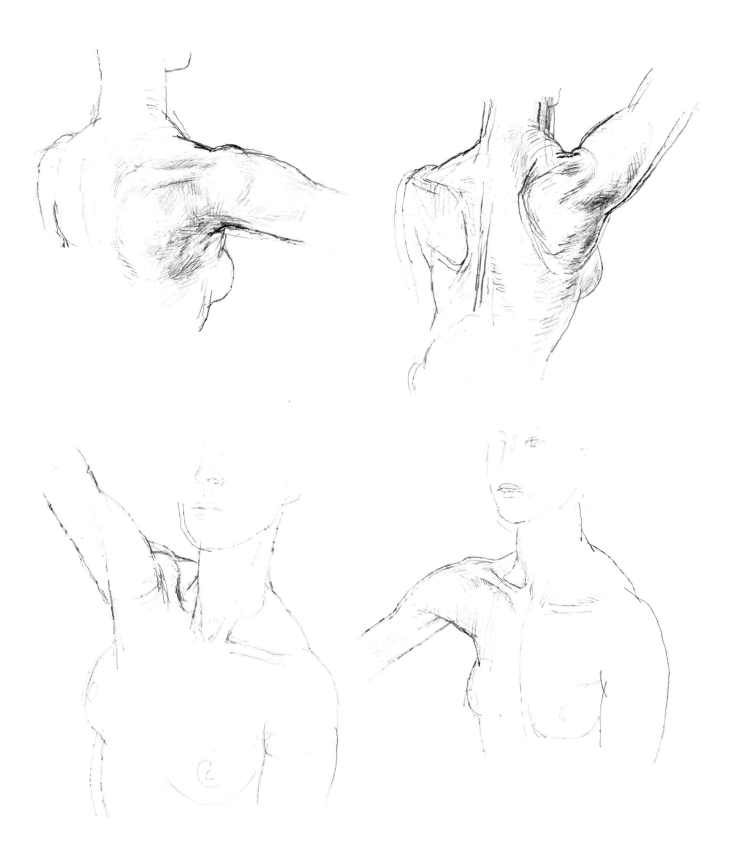

The arm

An arm in a position of support is very different in character from a hanging, relaxed arm. It is locked, straight at the elbow, with the shoulder usually high and the collarbone conspicuous.

Rotating the hand without moving the upper arm is made possible by the presence of two parallel bones (radius and ulna) joining the wrist to the elbow; the radius being on the same side as the thumb.

The leg and pelvis

The sartorius is the long muscle which goes from the iliac crest across the thigh to the inside of the knee. The division it makes can always be seen, leaving a familiar triangular shape on the inside of the thigh which is known as Scarpa's triangle. The anatomical and diagrammatical sketches which accompany the other drawings here help to explain the structure of the legs and pelvis.

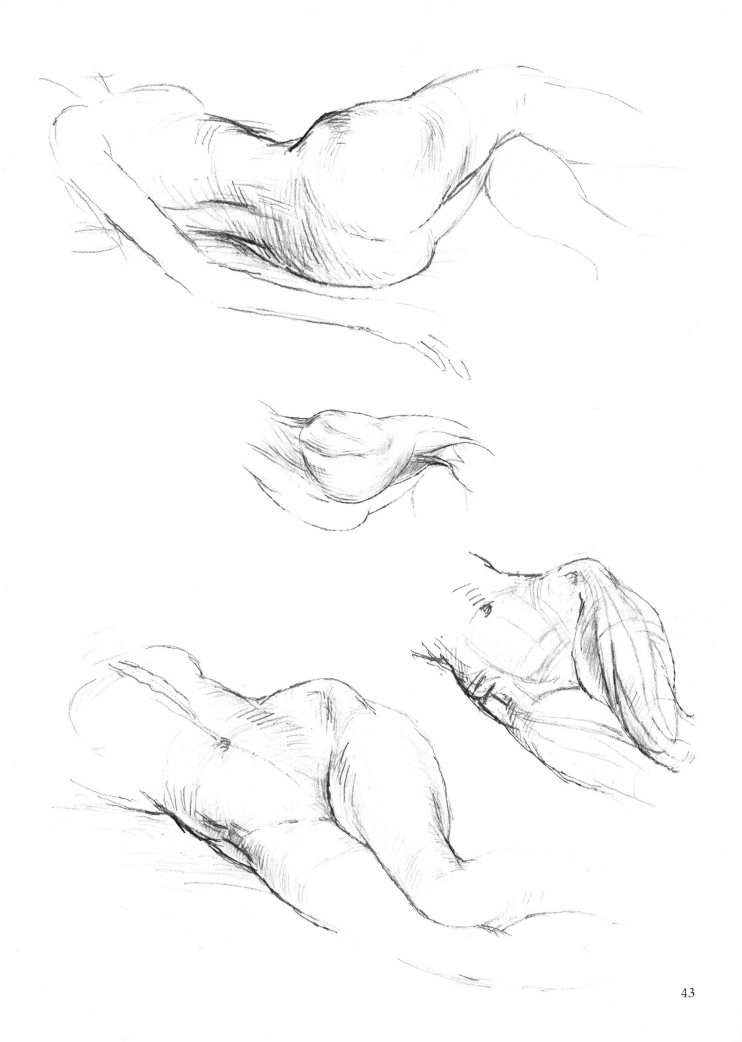

The head

Head and hands are the most expressive parts of the human body. The pose of the head often suggests the pose of the whole body and, with standing or seated figures at least, it is usually best to start with the head. Unlike many parts of the body, it has a fixed shape and size and so provides a constant to which other parts can be related.

The diagrammatic heads below show basic construction. Look for the main planes at right-angles to each other—front of face, side of cheek, top of head—in order to draw a solid rather than a mask. Draw the mass of hair, not the texture; hair, like a skull, has top and sides.

Fore- shortening

Foreshortening is a matter of drawing receding planes. It comes into any figure drawing to some extent, but does not always show itself as a problem. It is most difficult, obviously, when you try to draw a lying or reclining figure from one end. Careful measurement will help to make an accurate drawing. Plot the features of the head and body; then draw in the planes that connect them.

Lying

In a lying pose, the soft forms of the body collapse; the pelvis becomes very conspicuous and the soft waist small and flattened. Many parts are foreshortened, in particular the head. Always draw the supporting surface; if it has a strong, clear shape, draw it first and fit the figure onto it, particularly if the figure is lying at an angle.

In the bottom drawing opposite, notice how the soft forms of the female are distorted by gravity from their normal anatomical symmetry.

Sitting

Accuracy is less critical with a seated than with a standing figure, since the same exactitude of balance is not required. But try to make your drawing *look* right. Make several studies of the same pose from different viewpoints; a drawing from the side will increase your understanding of the front view and *vice versa*.

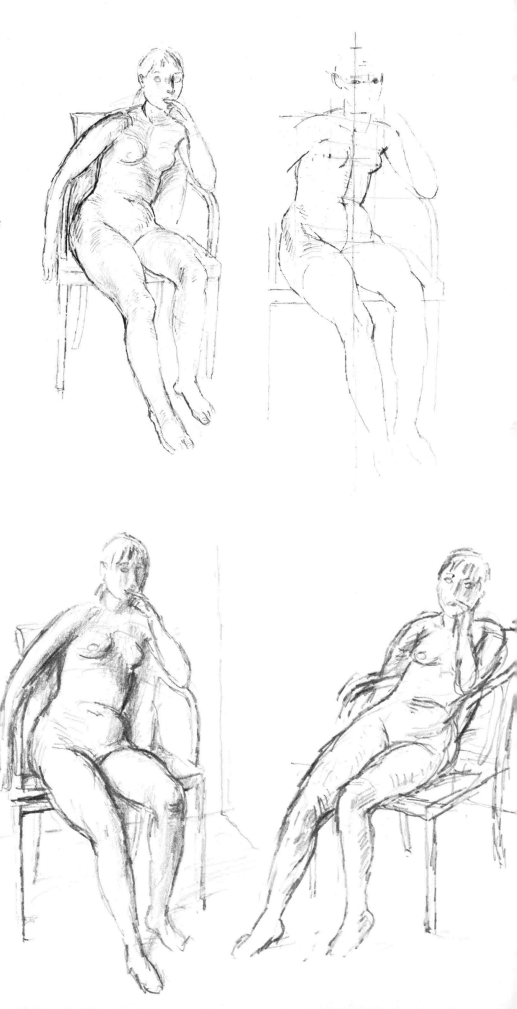

Drawing from memory

Many artists of the past and illustrators today learned the value of being able to do this. Memory of the body's articulation and of various poses are what is necessary. Memorising outlines is useless, since you are coping with mass and space. To start with, draw a box from memory—which is not difficult for anyone who understands its 3-dimensional shape and the planes that make it. Then draw a chair from the same ¾ view which was needed to show the box's shape. Finally, sit a figure on the chair.

It is helpful, first, to observe and sketch a model with a chair from several points of view in order to understand the pose and construction of your drawing. Make her stand, turn round, put a foot on the chair etc.

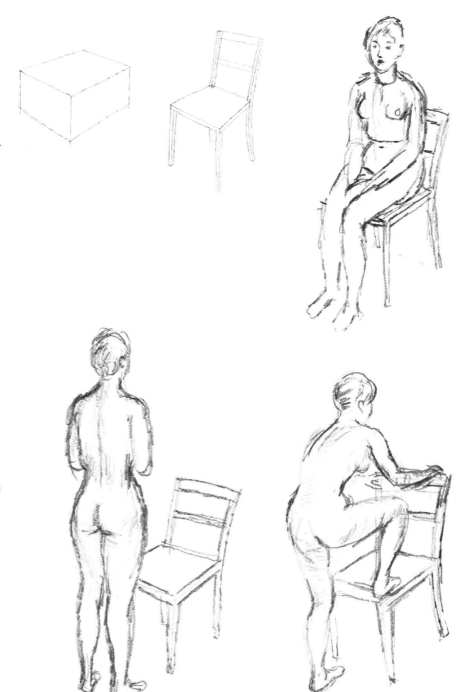

Line drawing

When making a linear drawing, look at the shape between the outlines not at the outlines themselves. The function of the lines on the paper is to suggest the volume which they enclose. Make sure the line has a feeling of direction and tension and that it relates to other lines in a way that implies the solid between them. If you draw a small freehand circle, and then another circle to suggest a ball, you will see what a line must do in a linear drawing.

Some poses lend themselves to line drawing more than others. In this one, the pose and front plane of the head is created by the position and drawing of the features.

The features of the face and torso make the front plane of this figure and imply its direction in space. The relationship of feet, shoes and chair legs imply the floor and the angle from which it is viewed.

Pen and pen-and-wash drawing

The firm and elastic Gillot 303 is a good nib to use. Obviously the ink must be waterproof, and I recommend neutral colours such as black or sepia, on white (also neutral) paper. The pen drawing and the wash should be done together, not separately, like two instrumentalists playing a duet. Do the fine work with the pen and put the wash on in areas, presenting the subject in broad areas of light and dark. It is wise to place your model where there is some fairly conspicuous light and shade.

A pen normally draws a fine line but, whether you use this or make a thicker one by pressing hard, draw vigorously to grasp the solid form. Indian ink is usually too thick and quickly clogs the pen. But if you dilute it—with distilled water—you can draw broadly without the dark areas looking like black enamel. In the pen drawing right, the planes and tones are indicated by cross-hatching.

The figure in its setting

Far more paintings have been made from drawings than have ever been done directly from the subject. You may wish to paint the nude from a drawing yourself, so get as much information about the surrounding of the figure as of the figure itself. As suggested earlier in this book, it is generally speaking a good idea to relate the nude to an environment; but this idea may be extended so that you have, for example, a picture of a room with a figure in it.

Composition

Design is important always. Before you draw, think about how your subject—figure and surroundings—will compose on the paper. Study the scene before you and decide on the boundaries of your picture. It may help to look at it through a rectangular hole cut out of a piece of card to the same proportions as your drawing paper.

Compositions often exist in terms of horizontals and verticals. In the sketch below the basic composition features are the vertical objects on the left which go from top to bottom, the horizontal couch and figure stretching to the right-hand boundary, and the vertical objects behind the figure.

In the drawing below, figure, plants, sofa and other objects have become fused together into a unified concept of form and light. Always try to draw links from one object in a drawing to another in order to bring unity into a composition.

Sketchbook

Art has its roots in observation. Cultivate this idea whenever possible by using a sketchbook. The model is equally interesting when she is resting or moving about between set poses. Make use of any opportunity to increase your understanding and extend your drawing ability.

61

Faces and expressions

John Raynes

Perspective and structure

The basic 'rules' of perspective outlined on page 12 are as relevant to drawing heads and expressions as to drawing anything else.

A head can be seen as a series of boxes, made up of the fairly flat planes or surfaces of its structure. These boxes—which are subject to the normal perspective rules—are not precisely right-angled, as the drawings here show; the plane representing the face, for example, is at 90° to the central axis of the head, but the head's widest part is towards the back, and the side planes therefore slope outwards from the front. The parallel lines positioning the facial features must be related to the perspective shape of the front plane—depending on your viewpoint. In perspective these lines will eventually converge, but on an object as small as a human head you will only notice the convergence if you approach very close, as in the more finished drawing opposite.

Having absorbed the idea of a head's box structure, try some drawings of a skull—either by copying other drawings like mine here or by sketching direct from a plastic model or real skull. You will learn from this how few formal differences there are between a skull and a living head. Once the spheres of the eyes are positioned and the nose completed by extending the bridge with cartilage (which also forms the nostrils), all that is missing to give the skull life is a comparatively thin layer of muscle and tissue covering the bones.

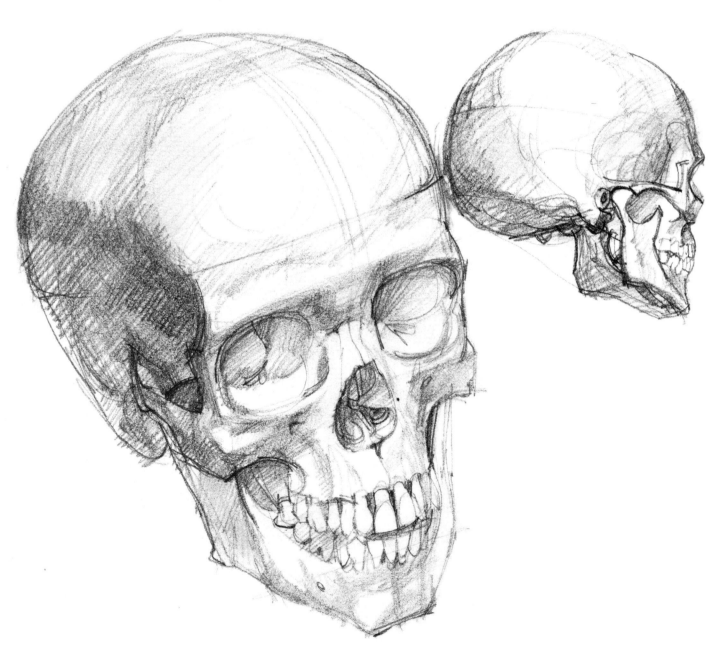

The only really strong muscle is the masseter which clamps the jaw shut: its bulks fills the space under the cheekbone (zyomatic), rounding out the angle of the jaw. All other muscles are muscles of expression (though some assist such other functions as speech and mastication too) and only need to be strong enough to pull the facial tissues into different shapes.

Except in very plump faces the bony structure is always evident—the cheekbone being particularly important. Every skull, like every face, is different; and only if you sense the skull beneath the skin of the living face you draw—and get its proportions right—will the soft features add up to a likeness of that particular person.

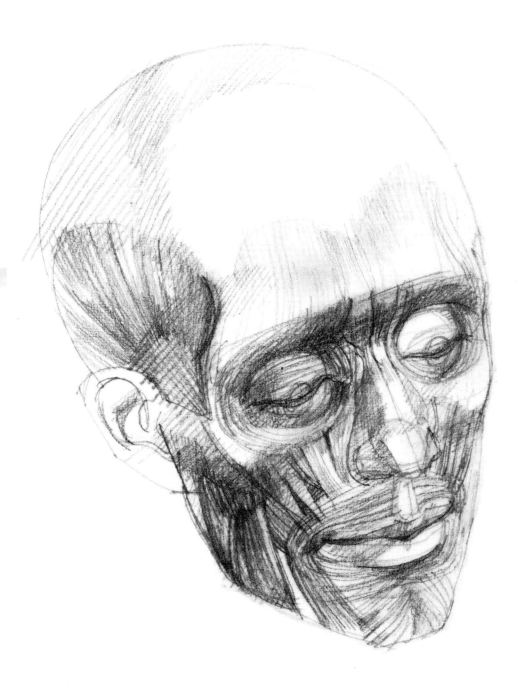

The drawings here show the changes in the structure of a skull and face brought about by the pivoting of the lower jaw when the strong masseter muscle is at work. Most people, when they open their mouths, tilt the whole head back as well as lowering the jaw. From a normal viewpoint, this exaggerates what you will notice anyhow—the angle of the jaw growing more extreme, the length of the lower face increasing, the mouth itself becoming extremely dominant.

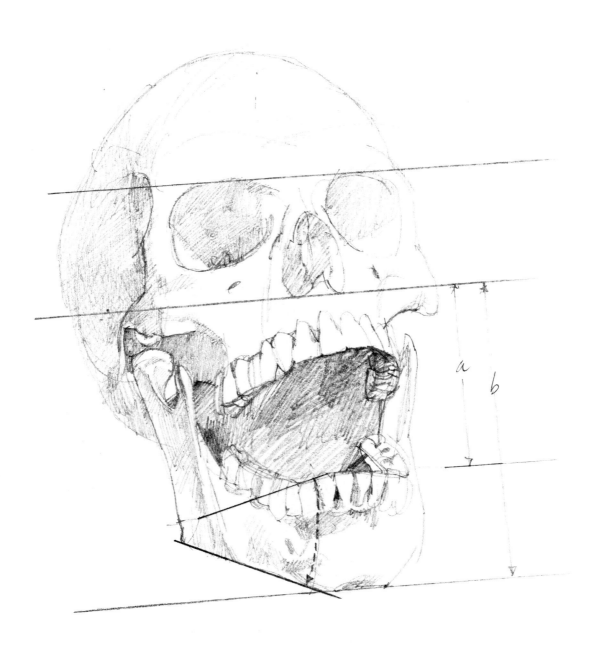

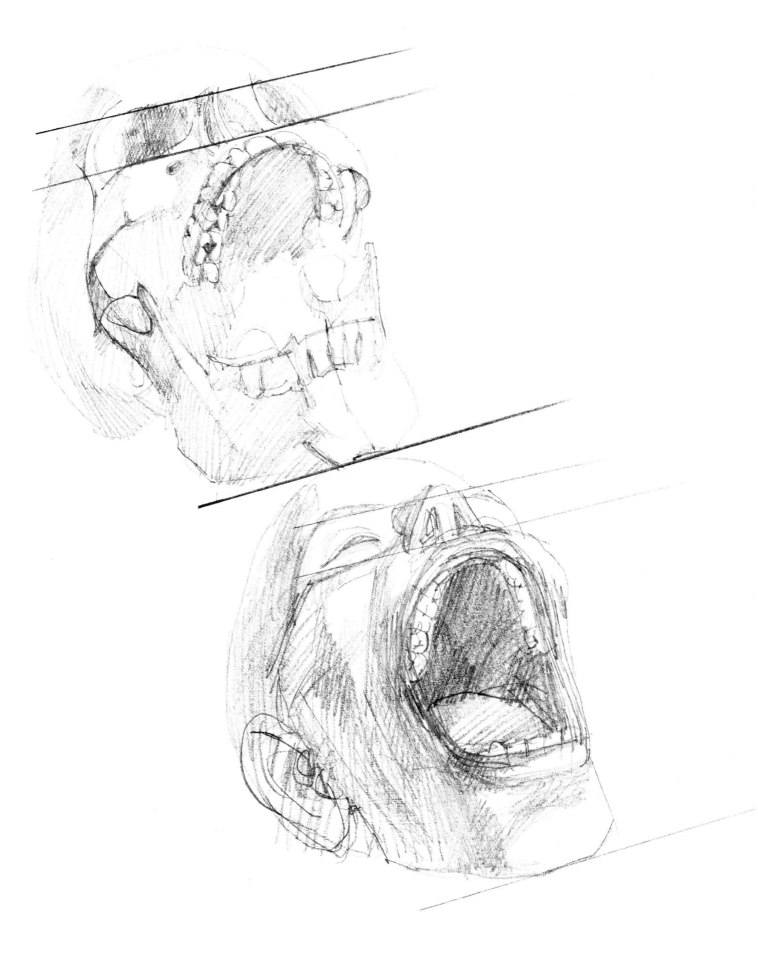

Where to begin

When you have made several drawings of skulls—becoming steadily more aware of the head's basic structure in the process—try studying a live face in repose, relating the soft, surface forms of the bones beneath.

First, spend some time arranging your model and setting up your own position. Drawing from life is made much easier if you can look from your subject to the drawing and back with a minimum of eye and head movement. For a right-handed artist, the best arrangement is illustrated opposite. The drawing board is upright on the easel, its sides parallel to the uprights of the room, and the easel is set just to the right of the sitter. If you are left-handed, reverse your position so that while working you do not have to look over your drawing arm.

If you prefer to sit, try to arrange things so that you can view your model directly over the top of the drawing board. But keep your board as upright as possible to give yourself a straight perspective view. On a tilted board a drawing easily becomes distorted, the details diminishing in size towards the top of the paper.

Step by step: repose

This is the first of three stages of a drawing of a subject with a relaxed non-expression. Note that the pencil has been used very delicately, my intention being to build up a grid of marks which work out where features are to go. It is a searching first sketch and, deliberately, no mark or line is so dark that it cannot be changed or drawn over.

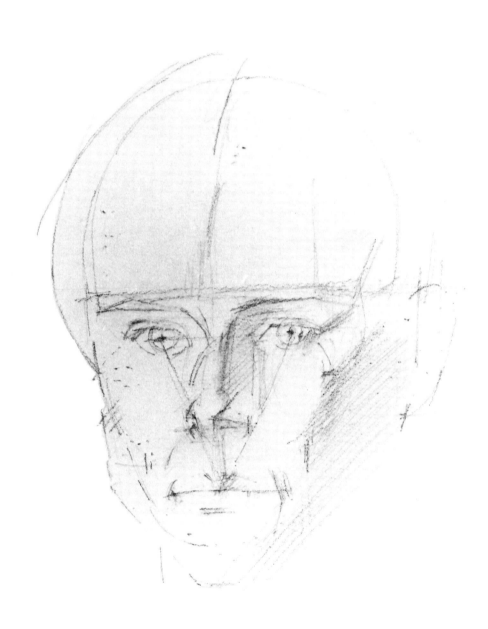

Here the search has been carried further and tone is creeping in. The word 'search' accurately describes what is happening, because anything may yet be changed. As your drawing becomes steadily more filled out, all earlier lines need to be continually questioned, so that the picture becomes both more finished *and* more correct at the same time.

This, the final stage of the drawing, shows that the policy of searching and changing as you continue to draw has been followed to the end.

Compare the finished drawing here with each of the previous stages, and notice where the earlier, exploratory lines have been modified as the drawing progressed. Remember that the relative positions of the features and the distances between key points such as the pupils of the eyes, the eyes and the tip of the nose, and the eyes and mouth, which were established in the first stage of the drawing, should be checked constantly.

Note also that the calm, relaxed expression of this subject is conveyed mainly in the eyes and mouth and by the general absence of tension in the facial muscles.

When you are making a portrait drawing, don't forget to let the sitter rest from time to time. If your model becomes stiff and uncomfortable, his or her expression is unlikely to remain relaxed.

Step by step: the frown

Since you tend to frown when you are concentrating, making a self-portrait is a good way to learn what frowning does to a face.

When drawing a mirror reflection, it helps to prop up your head (mine is supported here by hand and elbow) so that movement is kept to a minimum. My drawing board was on an almost flat surface just in front of the mirror, so that I needed to move only my eyes to see the drawing my right hand was making.

Again, before starting to draw, spend some time arranging the set-up. Experiment with the expression itself, too, choosing one that you can maintain consistently, and choose a position where the direction of the light will have most impact on the expression. A furrowed brow is probably best lit by a strong cross light. Here it came from a window on my left, so much of the front of my face was in half shade. The white paper reflected some light back on to the shadowed surfaces, providing a rich variety of tones.

As in the last sequence, the first stage (opposite) is a collection of exploratory marks, some of which are confirmed later, others ignored. Once again, nothing is erased, and the final picture is therefore a record of the exploration process as well as a finished drawing. Notice that spectacles have their own particular shape—which you can use to help define the position of the eyes and width of head, rather than trying to fit them round the face.

In stage two, some tone has
been added, as part of the
continuing search for the main
forms. The hand is treated as
though it and the face were one
form—which, for the moment,
they are. All parts of the
drawing proceed together.

As the drawing comes to completion, the forms are solidified, and the creases caused by the frowning expression gradually defined, both by lines and by interruptions in the tone covering most of the face. Creases make not only furrows of shade but also light-catching ridges.

The Smile: General

Like many expressions, a smile is difficult (or impossible) for a sitter to hold long enough for you to draw from life. A fleetingly-observed smile can sometimes be incorporated in a face reposing, and a gentle smile—particularly if part of a habitual expression of that person—can be held for a while before it looks strained. But a smiling face is very much more than one whose mouth has its corners turned upwards; and to understand *how* and *what* to draw, you really have to seek the help of photography.

Ideally, take several photographs of one person showing different expressions and notice how all the features change in each. Otherwise, study other people's snaps and photographs in magazines of smiling, laughing people, and learn from them to observe more closely the same expressions in real life.

The whole face is involved in a smile. The cheek muscles bunch into a clenched, rounded shape which pushes up beneath the lower eyelids, creasing the corners of the eyes, producing a familiar fold which links the nostril with the corner of the mouth. The corner of the mouth is therefore pulled outward, though not always upward. As the smile broadens, the mouth, stretched tight over the teeth, opens; and in the laugh, the jaw relaxes and the teeth part. At the same time the increased bunching of the cheek muscles narrows the eyes from beneath until, in an explosive laugh, they close almost completely.

The smile: female

The older woman here has obviously done a lot of smiling. Habitual clenching of cheek muscles has produced deep, permanent furrows radiating from the corner of bright, alert eyes. And although her lips are closed and not upturned at the corners, the whole face is lit with a smile. The younger head is similarly animated, but the smile isn't so warm, partly because the laughter lines have not had time to develop, but more because of a lack of eye-to-eye contact with the viewer. Almost always, if a smile is directed towards the artist (and therefore towards the viewer of the picture), it looks warmer and more personal; Leonardo's 'Mona Lisa' is an example.

Open-mouthed smiles require careful observation of teeth, especially upper teeth, as a *whole.* The entire dental arch must be drawn in correct relation to the frontal plane of the face, or the expression will seem strange and twisted. If you want a female smile to look dazzling, leave the divisions *between* the teeth unstated— merely suggesting them through the scalloped gum shapes between upper lip and teeth.

The smile: male

The same muscular mechanisms are at work on a male as on a female face, but the forms tend to be more angular, the folds more defined. The bony structure is heavier, especially at the brow ridge, the cheekbone and the lower jaw. This often results in deeper-set eyes, which narrow more readily in a smile, and more pronounced, less fleshy and rounded jaw and cheek muscles. The lips, too, are usually less fleshy, especially the upper lip, and only slightly deeper in colour than the surrounding skin tones.

Because teeth (like the whites of eyes) are white, any changes in tone they show are subtle in comparison with the tone changes on the surrounding face. So, unless you have worked out a full range of tones for the whole drawing, it is best not to define individual male teeth any more strongly than female ones. The stronger they *are* defined in a sketched drawing, the more attention you draw to them and the less benign the smile will seem.

Step by step: the smile

When speed is essential (which it is when trying to capture a smile from life), charcoal is a useful medium. You will get the most out of it by drawing boldly in broad areas of tone. And since you can make charcoal alterations easily, it isn't necessary to 'search' in quite the same careful way as described in previous step-by-step sequences.

Begin swiftly and strongly, remembering that the slightest touch with hand or cloth can modify the boldest marks. Use a putty rubber for complete erasure or to add highlights to dark areas as the drawing progresses.

The three stages here show a quick transition. The last one could have stopped earlier or gone on longer; *you* have to decide when you feel you have caught the expression and therefore when to stop.

Anger and aggression

A frowning brow is an obvious component of an angry face, but the mouth plays an important role too as the expression deepens from displeasure into active anger or aggression. When shouting is involved, the mouth often becomes square as the outer edges of the lower lip are pulled downwards and outwards.

The bottom drawings on this page show the exposure of lower teeth, which is characteristic of non-vocal aggression.

The two drawings here demonstrate how close an expression of anger may be to one of extrovert delight. Only the lower lip's outer edge and the eyebrow shape distinguish one from the other, the jaw opening and the bunching of cheek muscles being identical.

Sorrow

The traditional face of sorrow is exemplified in the theatrical mask of tragedy—the face of a tragic clown, with downward-sloping eyebrows and a mouth pulled down into an arc. Real life is rarely so extreme. The eyebrows often meet together in a frown. The mouth may adopt a variety of shapes, but a frequent feature is muscular bunching at its lower corners, which gives a grim set to the cheek (below, right). The fine pen drawing shows a grimace of pain.

89

Fear

The salient feature of the face of fear is the widely opened staring eye. Whether the eye opens to see more clearly that which is fearful, or to scare it away, is uncertain, but many animals stare similarly when frightened. Although the mouth may open too, it will be with a passive dropping of the jaw, not exposing the teeth—unless the fear is sufficiently extreme to produce a scream of terror.

If you light the face from below, the feeling of fear will be dramatised.

Other expressions

The human face is capable of many more expressions than the primary ones already described—combining the basic facial movements in a bewildering variety of permutations. Here are a few of them. The strained face below is that of a competing athlete; the others are self-explanatory.

Never assume symmetry in any of the features. The eyes, for example, are often very different from each other. The close-up (centre opposite) demonstrates that when eyes are turned sharply sideways, the one nearer to the object looked at is usually more open than the other and its pupil further from the corner.

93

It is not only the face that conveys an expression. The set of the head, attitude of shoulders, positioning of arms and hands, all contribute. In the drawing of the old woman opposite, the face itself contributes very little. Even when (in a three-quarters back view, for example) the face is almost hidden, an expression can be conveyed by the tension or slackness of neck and shoulders.

Watch how people use their hands to support, conceal and accentuate facial expression.

Old age

As a face ages, skin loses its
elasticity, muscle loses its tone,
and the creasing caused by
expression becomes permanent,
recording habitual moods and
attitudes to life.

Searching out these etched patterns is fascinating, but don't forget the underlying bone structure, which is often more evident in old age. Also look for fat deposits, which tend to concentrate around the jowls and neck but may also puff out around eyes and cheeks.

In old age the differences between men's and women's faces become less obvious; sometimes only the distribution of scalp and facial hair makes the sex identifiable.

Childhood

Here, by contrast, are some drawings of the rounded, unmarked faces of children.

Character has not yet emerged and the bones of the skull are not complete, but from its earliest months a child's range of expression is wide and vivid.

Final note

To draw expressions convincingly (as with drawing anything), you need first the develop and use your powers of observation, and then plenty of practice. Learn to look closely at the faces of all the people you meet, as well as those you persuade to pose for you, and try to understand, for example, what happens to the whole of the head, neck and even shoulders, when someone laughs or frowns. If you represent a frown simply by knitted brows and a downturned mouth, or a smile by crinkling eyes and a mouth turned up at the corners, your drawing will be little more than a cartoon.

Even if you observe carefully, you may not remember what you have seen. So carry a sketchbook with you whenever possible and try to put down on paper something—however sketchy or incomplete—of the faces and expressions you come across. Don't put down what you think *ought* to be there; draw only what you honestly see.

Study the drawings of established masters, in preference to those of contemporaries, unless you are sure of a contemporary's quality. There is some very good drawing about, and some very bad; time has sorted out the best of the past.

Children

Roy Spencer

Masses and planes

Many drawing problems disappear as soon as you realise that a picture is an *interpretation* of what you see, not an *imitation* of it. The first essential is to represent or imply solid form and space. Don't copy the tone of your subject; try to understand its solid shape as you would that of a cube, and use tone to make the forms you have observed.

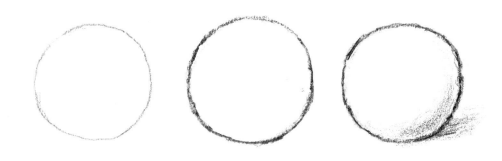

The first drawing here is a ring on the paper, drawn without any suggestion that it represents a solid. In the second, the line moves round as if it were enclosing a solid and implying the solid form. The third drawing has been taken a stage further: the addition of tone and a cast shadow make the object appear real and tactile.

Try a still-life subject, using as little tone as possible—suggesting the form with your lines. The line here is given meaning because I looked at the surface of the fruit rather than at the outline.

To make a linear drawing of a solid object, you must look for planes such as those shown in the bottom picture.

Tone and colour

Tone can be used to represent colour, as in the drawing here. The girl's dark hair and sweater, the colour of the cheques on her jacket and patterns on her skirt are all represented by different tones of grey.

The drawing opposite, on the other hand, is not concerned with colour of clothes or skin; the areas of light and dark represent the fall of light and shadow on the sitter.

103

It is important to distinguish between tone used to represent colour, and tone used to suggest planes.

In the picture opposite, the side of the girl's nose is dark and the front light, but the colour of side and front is the same. Tone has been used to show the planes which make the form of the nose. I could have described the form of the blazer in the same way but to do so would have made the drawing fussy, and the form of the face is more important to the picture than that of the blazer. The blazer's form is therefore *implied*, rather than *described*. Always draw with purpose. Each part of a picture must support the design as a whole as well as representing the appearance of the subject.

Be similarly selective when using tone to indicate colour. The shape and colour of hair or different garments can be as central to a drawing as the representation of solid forms. But look for an overall pattern and pay careful attention to it as your drawing proceeds. Pay attention also to the light areas among these colour shapes, which provide their own pattern. The paper on which your drawing is made sets the tonal 'key': light areas (even if they are far from white) are represented by the white paper in this drawing. All dark areas are relative to this whiteness; if you make them too black you may flatten the area rather than giving it an impression of form and reality.

Studies
in tone

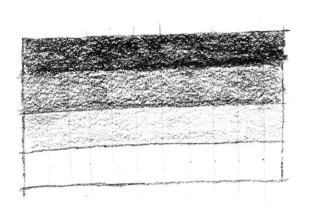
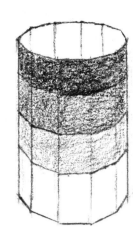

Divide a piece of drawing
paper into several bands. Make
the top band black and leave
the bottom one white. Darken
the middle bands in progressive
stages from black to white by
painting them with different
mixtures of black and white
poster paints. Then fold the
paper into vertical strips and
stick the ends together to make
a faceted cylinder as in the
diagram. Stand the cylinder on
a table in a side light and
observe how each plane
changes in relation to the
direction of the light. Big
changes occur in the white
band; comparatively small ones
in the black.

Next, make drawings of still-life
objects which include your
faceted tone scale. The more
you practise on inanimate
objects, the better equipped
you will be when you come to
draw children. A still-life
doesn't move; whereas a
young child rarely stays
completely still for more than a
few minutes (twenty if you are
very lucky). Drawing still life

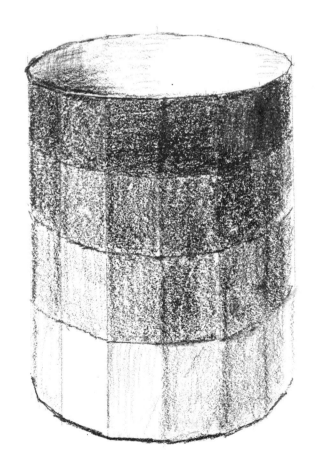

will teach you to understand form at your own pace, and the form of a child's head is not basically different from that of a fruit.

Fore-shortening

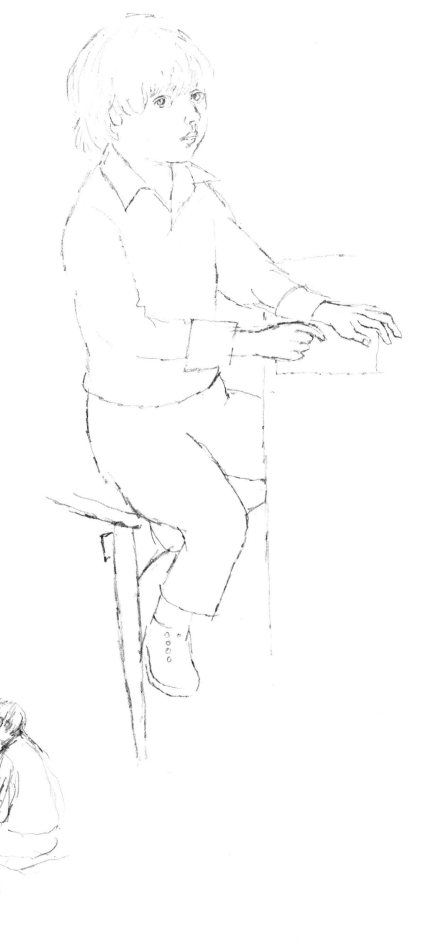

When drawing a child's portrait, sit only a few feet from your subject in order to see his features as clearly as possible. This will mean that the lower part of the figure is very foreshortened. Fixing some points by measuring against your pencil can help you, especially, to draw the pattern of the shapes. Foreshortening is particularly troublesome because the perspective becomes steeper and steeper, and the distortion can suggest a disproportioned figure. In the drawings here the chair is essential, in order to explain the geometry of the boy's legs.

The head

You will learn a lot from making several quick drawings of the same head. Get your sitter to turn away from you, drawing by drawing, until the nose has disappeared from your angle of vision.

Notice, in the drawings opposite, how foreshortened the nose is when the head is tilted back—the tip of it being brought very close to the eye.

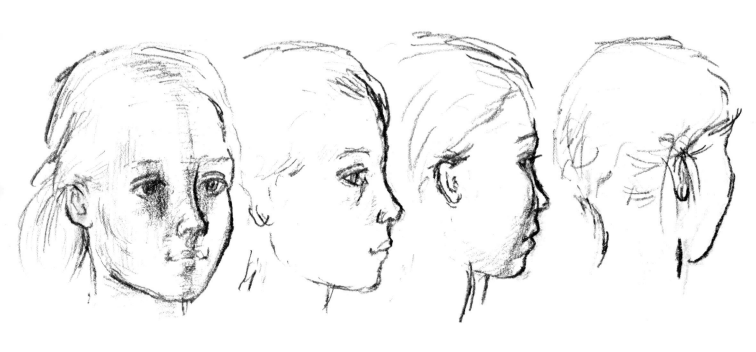

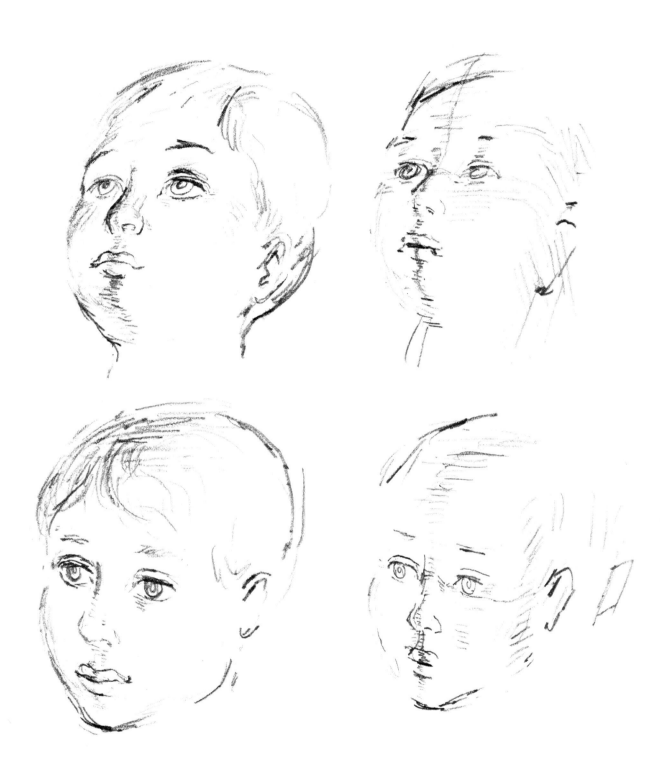

111

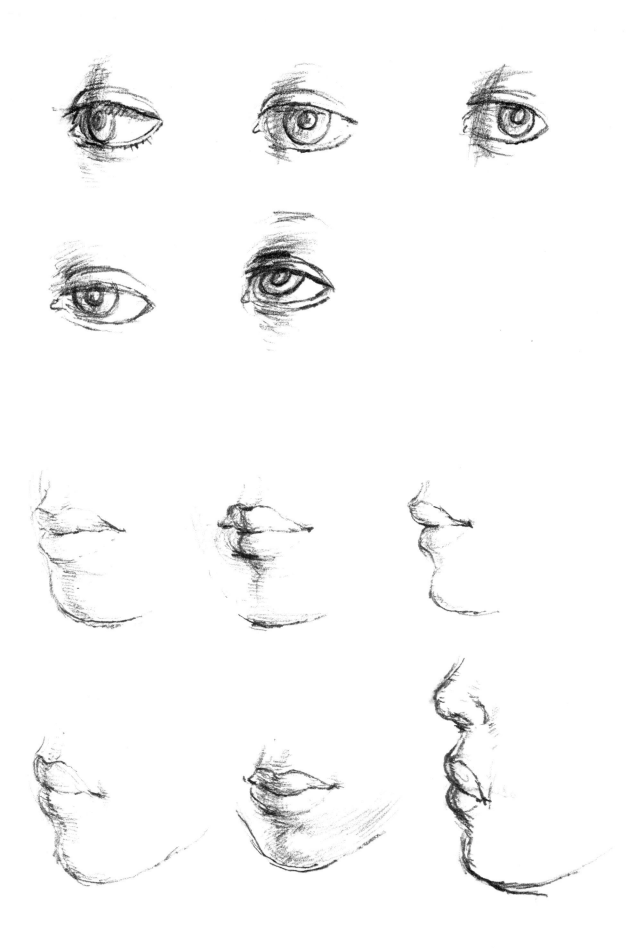

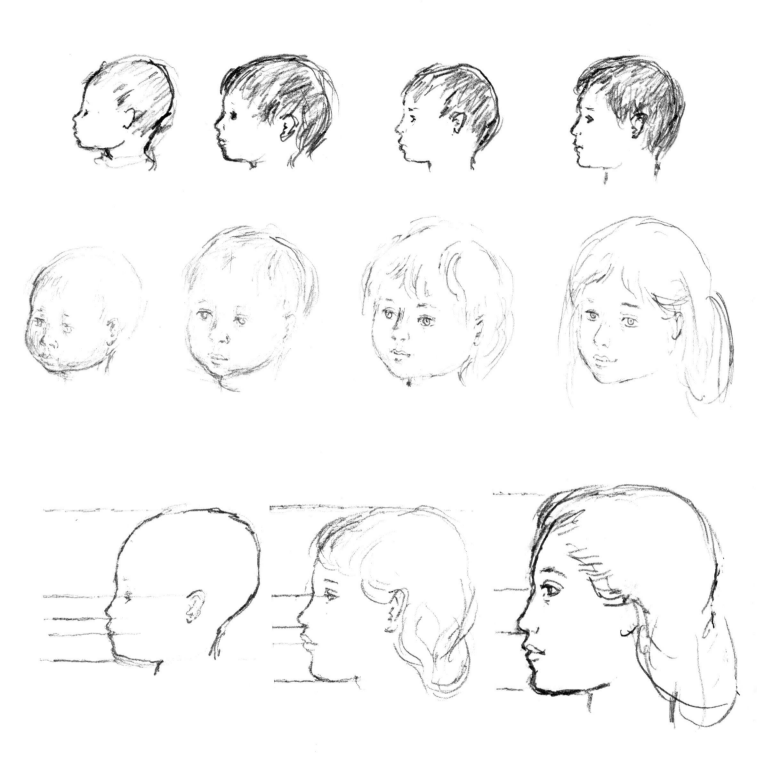

Draw eyes and mouths in several positions also—as in the sketches left—practising the tonal skills you learned from drawing still life.

Above: the two upper sets of drawings show the characteristic development of the head in the first ten years of a child's life. The lower set shows the characteristic head proportions of a baby, a ten-year-old and an adult.

Pen and wash

For a pen-and-wash drawing it is particularly important to have a subject who will sit still. Put him or her in a strong side light if you are a beginner, because it is easier then to understand the effects of light and shade. The tonal studies suggested on pages 106–7 are good experience for pen and wash, as for pencil and other media.

Use black waterproof ink and a paper that will absorb the wash readily; a non-absorbent paper tends to produce uncontrollable puddles. Use the pen for lines and the wash for areas. Don't try to 'model' with the wash; concentrate on where to put it rather than producing varieties of tone. If you understand the solid shape you are representing (pages 106–7), you will place the tone where it makes the form rather than copying the appearance of the subject.

First draw with the pen; then help the form you are making with the wash. Mix the wash as you need it in small quantities; a white saucer will show how dark it is. With the right paper, you will be able to work over the first wash after a few minutes. The incomplete head on the left indicates the procedure. For your first drawings in pen and wash, look for the pattern in the subject as a single dark tone against the light areas.

A baby

A subject as mobile as a six-month-old baby needs skill and directness of drawing. You may have to make many new starts, and will probably have several drawings on the go at once, on the same piece of paper. Get someone to hold the baby's attention in some way. Draw an eye and hope that he will resume the same position later so that you can draw the other one. Gradually, you will learn what the baby looks like and see your way to a complete drawing. In the final drawing (page 118) washes of colour were added and unnecessary lines taken out with process white.

A twelve-year-old

In contrast, the subject of this drawing was pleased to pose with squash racquet in his favourite outfit and controlled enough to sit still for half an hour or more. The younger child joined in voluntarily, dressed to suit.

Young children

When young children come
especially to pose, you must
start instantly. They are keyed
up for the occasion, but their
interest and co-operation will
last only a limited time. Each of
these children posed for about
twenty minutes. The 'extra'
from page 119 turned up again
for the left-hand drawing.

Make the most of a uniform,
putting in the various badges,
etc., and represent the colour
where you can. The child has
not dressed up for you to study
nuances of light and shade.

Older children

If your sitter is an older child, let her walk about and talk while you are getting ready to draw. She will be more at ease when she poses, and you will have had the opportunity to observe such physical characteristics as the shape of her head and such personal traits of stance and movement as how she holds her hands. Choose a pose which will display these characteristics and keep them in mind; it is easy to forget them when you are paying attention to such details as getting the corner of the lips right or the eye.

The two drawings on the right were in a sense trials. In the first, the dress was too casual and the model looked too old; the second is too heavy and the exuberance of the hair is missing.

If the sitter is to remain awake she must understand that, within reason, she can move when she likes. Once the pose is established, she can return to it quite easily.

At the age of fourteen, a co-operative sitter will stay still for quite a long time. This one chose her own clothes for the occasion, and her dark skin looked good against the light cream blouse. Her shoes and general grooming had a sophistication and individuality about them which required an elegant chair.

The drawing started as shown on this page: the eyes first, then the nose, cheek, lips, the hair indicated, the collar and tie. A measurement located the hands. As the drawing proceeded door-wards it was necessary to note the perspective, as shown in the lower drawing here.

The background to the figure was drawn in last. It is preferable, although not always possible, to have the figure there when you draw the background—even if she doesn't hold her pose—so that you can see the scale and relationship between them.

Children in movement

Here, the 'extra' from pages 119–20 came into his own.

You can only learn how to draw by drawing. Practise as often as possible, attempting to draw children whatever they are doing. You may never start if you wait for them to stay still. With young children, rapid drawing is essential. There is no time to model the form; you must imply it with line. The child on this page thought he was keeping the same pose while I made these three drawings.

Don't leave out the accessories; they are often related to the action and the pose, and help to explain both. If a pose is expressed in the fingertips, draw them first.

127

Dancing class

Dancing is a subject that tempts many artists and students, in spite of its difficulties. Children in a dancing class have particular charm. The artist's double challenge is to convey the rhythm of figures moving in unison, and at the same time the individuality of each child. The figures are rarely still, but movements are repeated many times; it is necessary to draw very much from memory.

129

Start by drawing one figure fairly carefully, rather than rushing after several almost disassociated figures. Then (since your drawing is of a room with figures in it) sketch in the space of the room. Wherever figures appear in the room, try to draw them quickly in this place in the picture, concentrating on size and perspective. In more detail, draw the dancing mistress, the pianist and the children when they rest. Pay attention to the room itself. Its height, space and decoration help to set the scene and give scale and meaning to the figures. And, even if your drawings of the children are slight, you will end with a picture which has space and movement and in which you have attempted all that the subject offers.

Portraits

Benedict Rubbra

To draw portraits successfully you must learn to select important shapes and lines, to see and understand a complete form and to make your pencil describe what you see. (This section of the book is primarily concerned with pencil drawing—most of the examples were done with a 2B pencil)

You cannot draw a form unless you understand it. The shapes and forms must first be analysed.

The first thing to do, therefore, when you start to draw a portrait is to discover the lines and shapes that you can clearly understand.

The head is a three-dimensional object made up of rounded forms and different planes or surfaces. The contour, or outline, that you see is not the edge of a flat shape but the point at which the form turns away from you and disappears from view.

Don't make the common mistake of thinking that you will achieve a likeness just by getting the eyes, nose and mouth right. It is the varying shapes between the features, the total shape of the head, the quality and texture of hair and skin, that make one person distinct from another.

Select those things that *you* feel are relevant. A portrait must convey your idea of the person. It is what you choose to put in and what to leave out that will bring the portrait to life.

Look at the portrait opposite. Note the pose, the relationship of the set of the head to the shoulders. The three sketches on the left will help you understand the form and character of the subject.

1. This shows the upright position of head and shoulders and the simplified contour of the cheek and jaw in contrast to the soft shading within the face. The solid character of the subject is emphasized by even line and tone.

2. Uneven emphasis of line can change the quality of form.

3. A reminder of the characteristically solid form of the head.

Proportion

There are certain basic proportions. If you know these, you can watch for how and when they vary.

A frontal view can be divided by a grid (a). On an average head the distance from eye centre to eye centre is equal to the distance from the bridge of the nose to the mouth. The tip of the nose (where you see the highlight) falls half-way between the bridge of the nose and the mouth; this distance will fit six times vertically and four times horizontally into the area of the head.

There is a fixed relationship between the centre of the cheek bone, the centre of the ear and the base of the skull. These three points form a straight line, and the ear is the half-way point (b). Note the relative position of the ear to the highest point of the head and how the profile is divided into six parts as in (a).

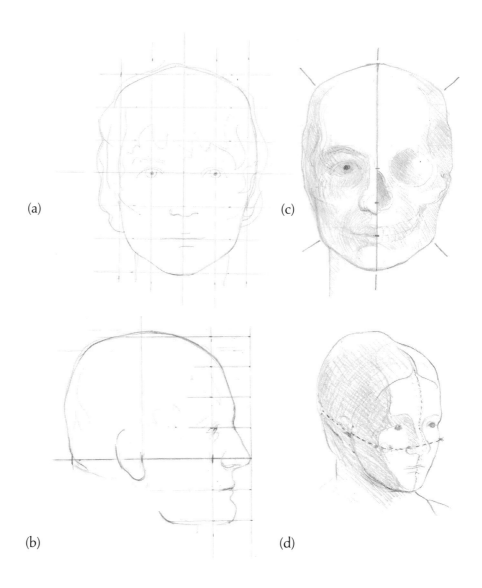

(a)

(c)

(b)

(d)

Notice where the main contours change direction and the relative positions of these changes; and how the forms of the forehead, cheek and jaw flow into each other. Make your eye travel across these forms. Try to understand the characteristic forms and shapes of the whole ((c); opposite).

Visualise the two aspects, front and side, as one three-dimensional form ((d) opposite). Notice how the outer contour of the cheek repeats itself on the inner side, where the tone changes. This contour indicates the forms of the face, and plays a very important part in portraiture.

Whatever the position of the head, the relationship between the cheek, the ear, and the base of the skull remains constant. Notice, below, how the line linking these three points tilts as the head tilts, when looked at from the side, on diagrams (a) and (b). Then note the relative positions of the eyebrow to the ear when the head is tilted forward (c) and of the mouth to the ear when the head is tilted backwards (d).

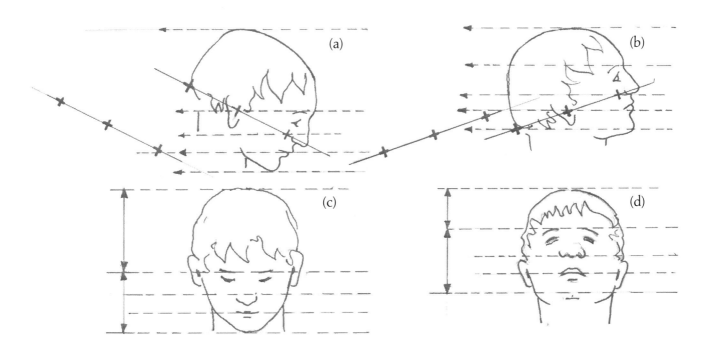

These positions will be the same when seen from the front (c and d), but because the head is tilted towards or away from you the horizontal proportions will be foreshortened—particularly the distance between the eye and the chin and between the eye and the top of the head.

See how the simple shape of a cup changes according to its position—this will help you to understand how the head can change shape in the same way.

You must always be aware of the position of your eye in relation to the subject. Make a note, for example, of the exact position of the sitter's ear and eye and use this reference, if necessary, to re-adjust your own viewpoint accurately.

Using your pencil

Practise making your pencil describe what you have seen and understood.

(a) Vary the thickness of the line. Treat the form nearest to you (e.g. the chin) with a richer and thicker line. The part of the drawing that is emphasized will appear nearer because it is noticed first.

(b) Draw the nearest part in detail and treat the rest with a softer broken line. The quality of the line makes a three-dimensional form.

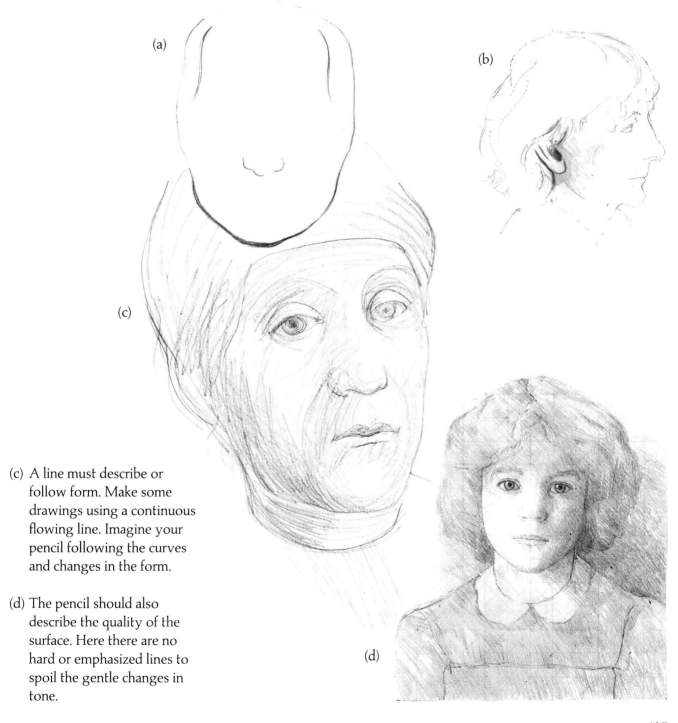

(a)

(b)

(c)

(c) A line must describe or follow form. Make some drawings using a continuous flowing line. Imagine your pencil following the curves and changes in the form.

(d) The pencil should also describe the quality of the surface. Here there are no hard or emphasized lines to spoil the gentle changes in tone.

(d)

Look for different characteristics and vary the way you draw and the medium you use accordingly—charcoal for a simple statement about tone, pen and ink for a crinkled texture.

Experiment with your pencil. Try mixing pen and pencil. Use the side of the pencil as well as the point. Note the other variations of texture below—a kneaded eraser has been used to vary the tone.

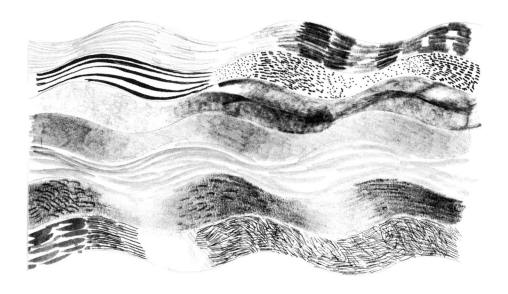

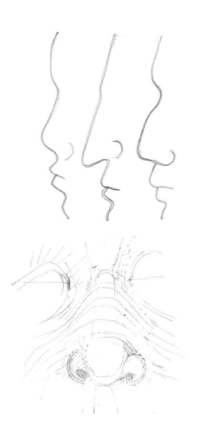

Study the profile to see the relative angles of forehead and nose and how much the nose dips in at the bridge, and also the curve from the underside of the nose to the upper lip.

Notice particularly the different planes and the characteristic way the form flows into the cheek and round the eye socket (left).

One of the most characteristic features of the nose is the way the forms move down from the forehead and into the eye socket. Notice how these forms have been 'felt' with the pencil, below.

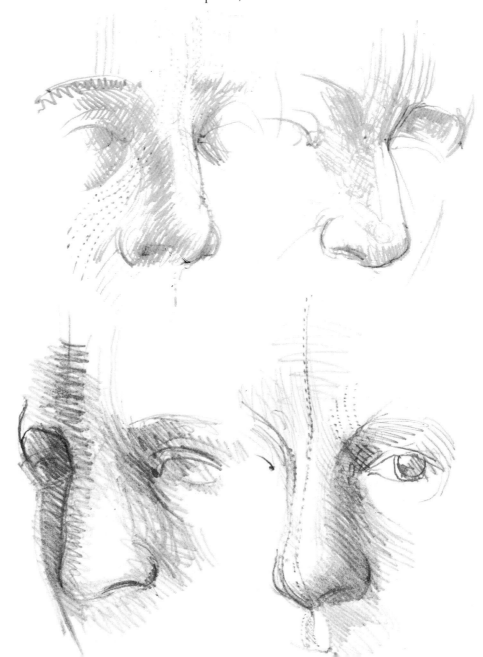

Placing yourself and your sitter

Place your easel as near as possible to your subject so that you can look from drawing to subject without much head movement. There should be plenty of space between you and the easel. If you are left-handed, have the paper or easel to the left of the sitter, otherwise your drawing arm will block your view. (See pages 68–9.)

Your sitter will find it easier to keep still if he or she has a comfortable chair with a straight back.

Keep the background simple—if necessary place a piece of plain card behind the sitter.

Decide on your eye level. Is it to be above or below the level of the centre of the sitter's face? Ask yourself whether looking slightly up at or slightly down on the sitter would make a more characterful drawing. If you look down on the head the shape of the face becomes elongated, even though the proportions are foreshortened.

It is worth spending time adjusting your position in relation to the sitter before you start drawing. Note the position of ear and nose and how much of the nostril is in view. Fix the point where the contour of the shoulder joins the chin or neck. (This is easier if the sitter wears something with a simple neckline.) Notice how this point varies on the two positions illustrated opposite.

Looking for the complete shape

Once you have become reasonably familiar with your pencil you will be able to decide how to use it according to the person you are drawing.

Look for the characteristic shape of the head. Here are three views of the same head. A simple line describes the contour.

If the contour is toned in, the head can be seen as a solid shape. The line has lost its importance and the tone makes the shape. Note also the shapes left by the white paper.

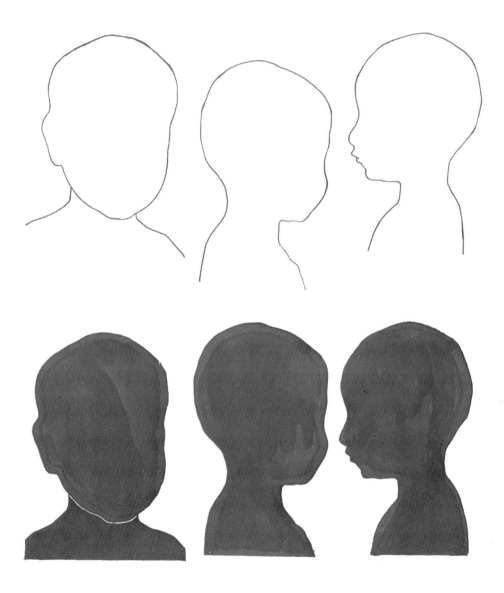

Pin a piece of paper behind the subject, large enough to cover the area of the head, with a network of diagonal and vertical lines drawn on it. Divide your drawing paper in the same way before you start drawing. Place yourself so that you can see a vertical line touching a point on the head and always refer back to this position. Now start drawing the contour, noting the points at which the diagonal and vertical lines meet the head.

Try placing the subject in front of a window and concentrate on the dark shape or silhouette. Now try and describe the shape by looking for the points where the contour changes direction, and make a series of drawings using only straight lines based on these changes of direction.

Light

Use the direction of light to emphasize the characteristic forms of the head.

These three drawings show how light from different directions (indicated by the arrow on the same heads seen from above) can reveal different aspects of the head. All the surface forms away from the light should be first toned in without drawing anything in detail. Remember that a sudden change of tone will indicate a sudden change of direction in the form and a gradual change of tone will convey a smooth or gradual change of direction (below).

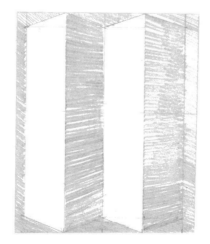

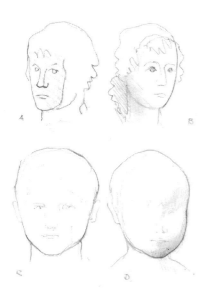

A characteristically square head with light from the side (top, left).

A soft front light for a gentle, oval face (top, right).

A bland, even light for a wide open face (bottom, left).

Light directed from above to emphasize the fullness of a child's cheeks (bottom, right).

Never have too strong a light on your sitter or the forms will become confused by shadows. If possible, use a constant north light. The problem of changing sunlight falling on the subject can be solved by hanging a white sheet over the window. This will diffuse the light without reducing it.

Light from both sides emphasizes the fullness of the jaw line.

A very useful light, slightly from above and to one side just catching the cheek of the dark side. Notice how the dark area has been blocked in without drawing anything in detail.

145

Choosing a pose

Choose a pose that is both characteristic and animated. If your sitter is slumped in a chair, looking straight ahead and with no turn of the head on the shoulders, your drawing will be dull.

Consider the position of the head and neck in relation to the shoulders. Look at the simple form of the neck and realize that it is cylindrical. See how the contour of the shoulder flows from the neck, and notice the spaces formed by the line of jaw and shoulder. Think of the head and neck as one continuous form. Always relate the position of the centre of the base of the neck to the chin.

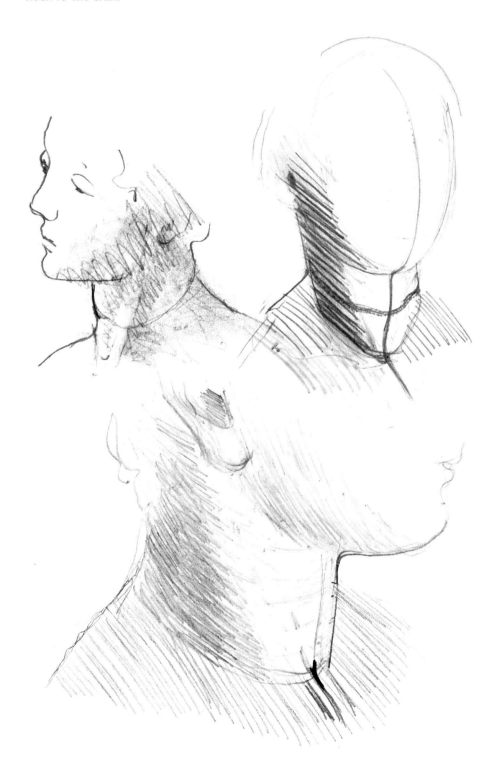

The way the eyes are directed in relation to the turn of the head and shoulders will add considerably to the animation of the pose. Look at these different poses of the same person. Note the turn of the head; the shoulder line in relation to the chin or cheek and the direction of the eyes; and the slope of the shoulders and thrust of the chin. Notice whether the eyes are looking in advance of the turned head or in a contrary direction.

Pose your sitter in different ways until you find the most characteristic pose. Avoid a pose that will be difficult to keep for any length of time. In any case, be sure to let your sitter rest at regular intervals.

Profile

You may decide that the most characteristic aspect of your sitter is the profile.

To achieve a likeness in profile, you will need very accurate observation and skilled control of your pencil.

The slightest variation in the thickness and emphasis of line will change the appearance. Avoid simply following the contour without first understanding the complete shape.

Use your pencil lightly, and gradually build up the contour and forms. In this way you will avoid a heavy, confused line.

Study a head turning into the profile and note the changing space between the cheekbone and eye and the contour of the nose.

Remember that a profile is a three-dimensional form. Look for the points nearest to you (cheekbone and ear) and follow with your pencil the forms of the jaw. The sketch below shows how the roundness of this contour is formed. Watch for relative positions on a vertical (eye and mouth) and the direction of the line from forehead to nose and nose to chin.

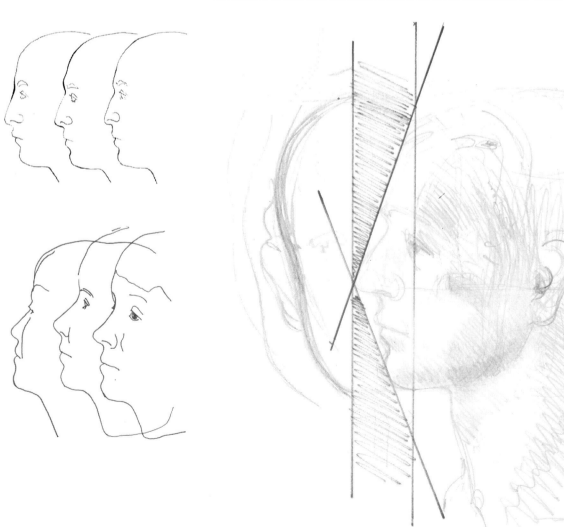

Pin up a square of dark card behind the sitter, large enough to cover the area of the head. Adjust your position so that the vertical edge of the card just touches the tip of the nose. Look for the background shapes, the proportions, and begin to feel for the form of the cheek.

Build up the contour with a gentle broken line. Establish relative vertical and horizontal points.

Concentrate on the main dark areas, looking all the time for shapes. Adjust your position if necessary to keep the original pose (in this pose you can just see the lid of the far eye).

Soften or erase unwanted lines by pressing with a kneaded eraser.

Vary the quality of the line. Notice the shape of the eye and how it is foreshortened when seen from the side.

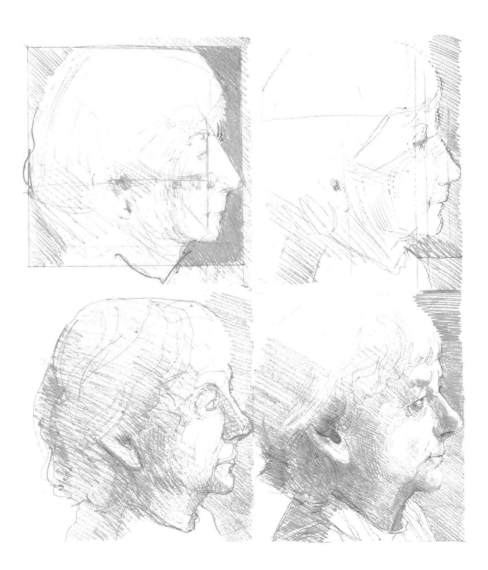

Three-quarter and full face

Note what happens to the perspective of the front of this box when it is turned to the side:

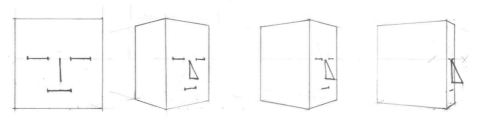

The same changes take place when a head turns from profile through three-quarters to full face. The drawing below illustrates these changes, using a very simple line and a contrasting background. Note particularly how the distance between the outside corners of the eyes becomes longer and the distance from the corner of the eye to the ear becomes shorter.

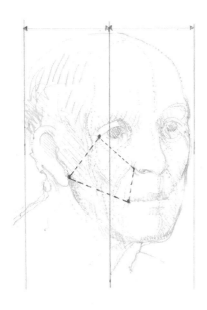

Begin the three-quarter view by fixing the position of the nearer eye. The drawing on the left shows how it falls half-way across the width of the head. (See page 134 to help you establish relative distances.)

Make a study of the relative positions of the four points surrounding the cheek bone. Discover how the shape of the cheek bone and jaw form the contour. Feel the forms with a gentle line. Note the position of the chin in relation to the neck.

Understanding the contour of the three-quarter view plays an important part in portrait drawing.

Avoid a heavy and unvaried line as it will flatten the form. Observe carefully the shaded areas here. Look at the shape of the foreshortened mouth and note how a variation in the contour changes the appearance. Notice the difference between the form and contour of the two noses.

Study also how the jaw line is formed. Think of the rounded forms flowing into the forms of the neck. Don't make the mistake of drawing the jaw with a solid hard line.

In a full face drawing the jaw line must be treated as the contour of the three-quarter view. Again, avoid a heavy, unvaried line. You can usually see some reflected light on the jaw. Never exaggerate this—darken the whole area, then increase the depth of tone surrounding the jaw line until it appears to lighten.

The right-hand pose below has more life than the one on the left. The head is turned away and the contrasting tone of the background heightens this tension.

Features: eyes

You have seen the importance of understanding the complete shape of the head and finding its characteristic variations. Now you need to fit the features within the shape. The most dangerous trap in portraiture is to suppose that a likeness depends on the features alone. It is the shape between the features and how these and the features fit within the head that create the likeness.

To position the eyes correctly, look for the important relative distances (a). (See also page 134.)

(a)

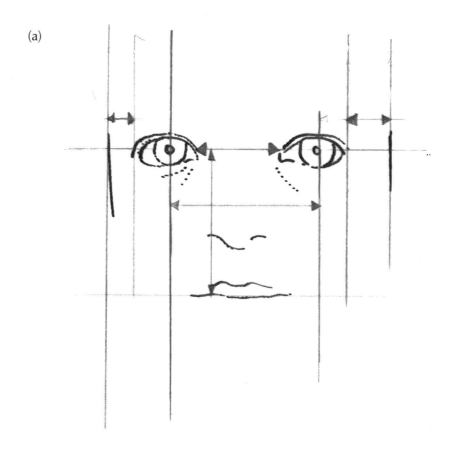

(b) 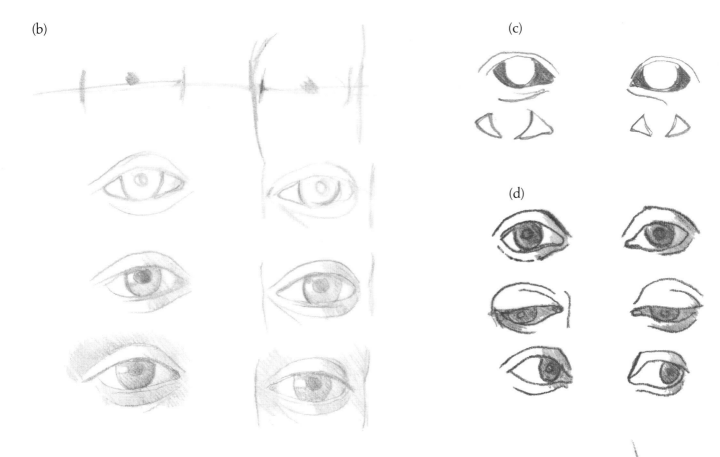 (c)

(d)

Watch for how much of the eyelid is visible (b) and the different shapes of the white areas (c). Indicate the rounded form of the eye by darkening the side away from the light. Then build up the variations of tone surrounding the eye. It is very important to indicate the overall tone of the iris and the character of its outline. Notice how the eyes change shape according to the direction of the gaze (d).

The fleshiness of the skin surrounding the eye, and the angle of the iris, both give character to the eye (e).

As you are drawing the eyes, keep checking relative distances and remember to give equal attention to the surrounding forms of cheek, brow and nose. Note the shadow cast on the iris by the eyelid (f).

(e)

(f)

153

Features: mouth

The mouth should be seen as part of the surrounding area and the chin. Study the form of the mouth and chin in profile. Never make too definite a line where the lip colour changes to skin colour. It is easy to over-emphasize this tonal change. Think constantly of the form flowing from the lips to the surrounding areas.

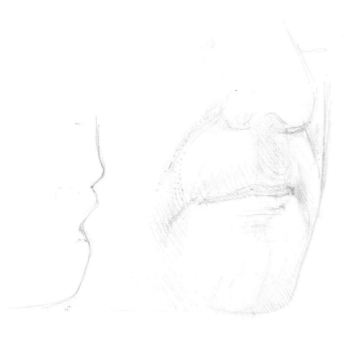

Feel for the forms with your pencil. Determine the direction of the mouth and its size in relation to the nose.

Draw round the lightest areas to develop the form of the lower lip and chin. Avoid using a hard line to delineate the lips and the division between them.

Find the shapes of the darkest areas (e.g. the corner of the mouth) and develop the variations in tone. Remind yourself continually of the changing direction of the surrounding forms.

Look for variation in the line along the centre of the mouth. The quality of this line shows the character of the mouth.

The form of the lips and the area between the top lip and the nose are important. Always note the characteristic shape and never exaggerate the variations of tone within it.

Features: nose

This drawing illustrates how the forms of the features fit into the forms of the head.

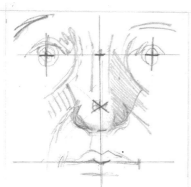

Remember some basic proportions—eye centre to eye centre, bridge of nose to mouth, tip of nose to bridge and to mouth—and how they relate to the whole head.

Exercises

Here are some simple exercises to encourage you to see one thing in relation to another.

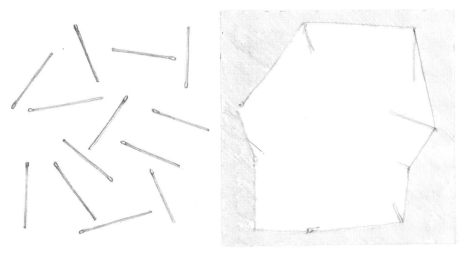

1.   See how well you can draw the relative positions of a random collection of matches.

2.   Work out the overall shape of the group.

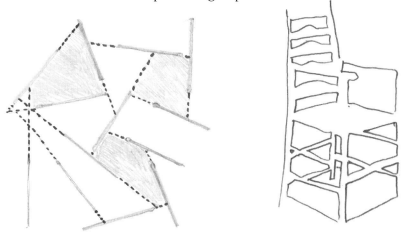

3.   Continue the direction of each match and see how many shapes can be made by the intersection of these lines.

4.   Draw the shapes of the space you can see through an object such as a chair.

5.   Draw a group of objects with a continuous line, making your eye move rapidly from side to side as you draw.

6.   Practise rapid drawing without taking your eye off the subject.

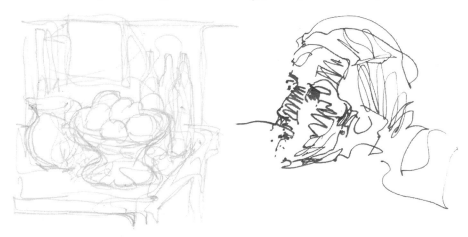

Hair

Never think of the hair as individual strands. Think of the total shape and how the contour follows the main changes in direction of the skull. Look for the quality of the hair and vary your use of the pencil accordingly.

Fair hair with the light areas contrasted against a dark background.

The solid mass of dark hair. Hard lines on the contour will spoil the effect of softness.

Block in the general tone of the hair. Accentuate the light areas by increasing the depth of the dark areas. Finally use a kneaded eraser to draw the few highlights.

Note the way different types of hair fall into smaller shapes. These shapes will have light and dark areas.

Vary the line to emphasize the quality of the hair.

Expression in portraits

Expression is caused by fleeting changes in the face, so in a portrait never attempt to draw an expression. Instead, as the drawing progresses, notice the characteristic ways in which small changes take place when your sitter is talking or thinking, and when you consider that your drawing is nearly completed make some final adjustments to the features.

Note the different treatment of the lower eye lid and the mouth in these three drawings.

Look for any changes in the surface forms of the brow (left, above), the sparkle in the eye (left, below) and the related expression of the liquid eye and slightly open mouth (below).

Watch the movement of the eyebrows; you may need to emphasize the nostrils and the surrounding froms.

When a smile begins (below) the contour of the cheek changes and the lower eyelid is pushed up.

Notice the shape of the dark areas of the nostril.

Self portrait

The main problem with a self portrait is that you cannot see your reflection and the drawing simultaneously, so you have to remember what you see.

With your head moving continuously from drawing to reflection it is difficult to keep re-establishing the same pose.

Choose a pose, then note the position of the iris, the distance from the corner of the mouth to the point where the neckline and cheek line join, and the relative distances A and B. These are foreshortened planes and the tendency is to exaggerate them and so make the head too wide.

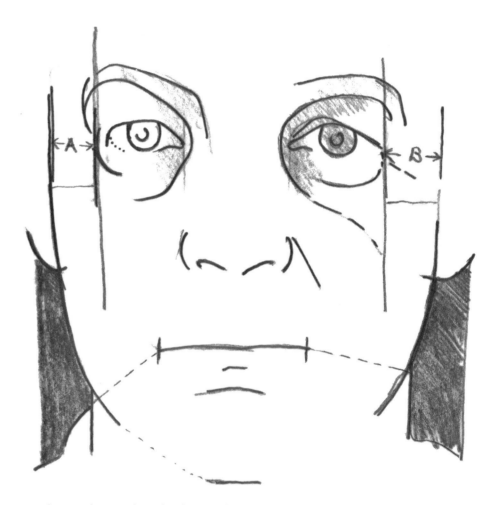

Mark your face with eight dots and note their relative positions when you have fixed your pose. Imagine lines joining the dots and the shapes that these lines would make. The drawings opposite show how these shapes will change as the position of the head changes. Note the very important direction of the line between the dot on the cheek and the ear lobe; and the relative position of nose and ear depending on the tilt of the head.

Every time you look at your reflection, check and re-establish these points of reference.

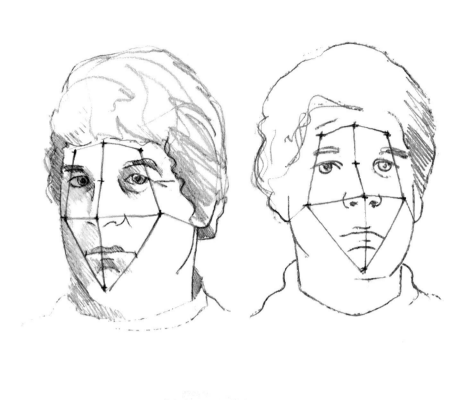

Pay particular attention to the shapes surrounding the eyes and the shapes of the whites of the eyes.

The easiest trap to fall into is to concentrate only on small areas.

Refer back to the pages on features, hair and the use of the pencil, and see how all these points are tackled in the finished drawing opposite.

Copying and other aids

Remember that a good portrait likeness depends on accurate drawing. You must see and understand the whole form and all the relative positions of the features.

Practise your technique of seeing and discovering by drawing from a bust. Draw it from as many unusual angles as possible; use unusual lighting and different media.

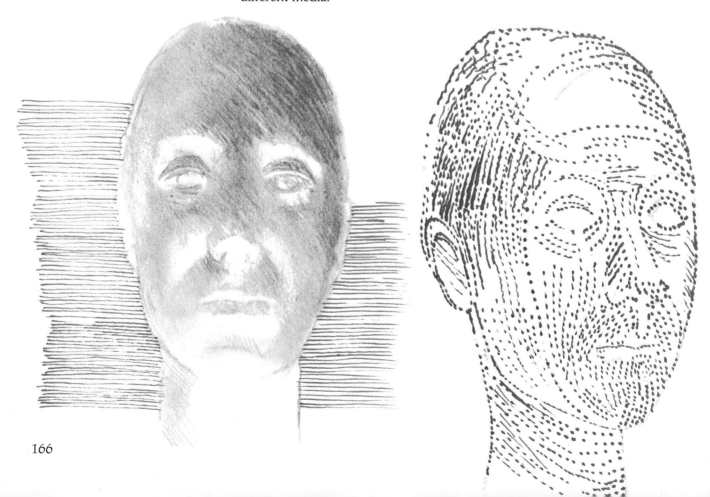

You can learn a lot by copying drawings by the great masters. Ask yourself what they have selected to draw and what they have left out.

Do not overwork a drawing. A finished drawing does not have to describe every aspect in great detail.

Try copying on to glass, to help you understand basic shapes and proportions. Place the glass between yourself and the sitter. Trace the main outlines and then the positions of mouth, eyes, etc. Use a fine felt pen. Keep your head very still and draw with one eye closed. It will take a lot of practice. Draw a grid over the drawing and then transfer it on to paper.

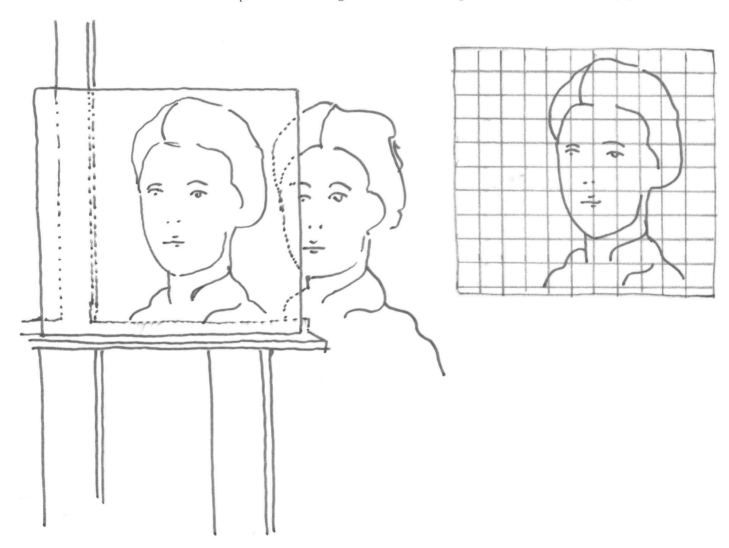

Hold up a stick in front of your subject with your arm outstretched. Make two marks to correspond with the position of the eye and mouth. Make two or three more marks on the stick at equal intervals, hold up the stick again and note where these marks fall on the head. Then turn your hand through 90° and compare these distances on the horizontal.

Make similar marks or knots on a weighted thread (plumb line). Move your arm from side to side, noting all the relative points on the vertical.

(Both these operations must be done with one eye closed.)

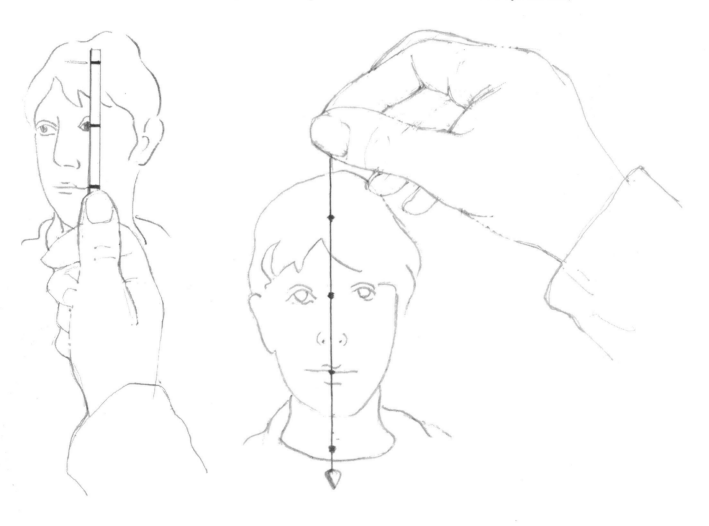

Racial types

Variations in the shape of the skull cause different types of face. Before you begin a drawing—say of an African—analyse the shape of the skull and try to imagine its profile. Use the plumb line to relate points on the vertical.

See how the shape relates to a square.

There are enormous variations within each racial type.

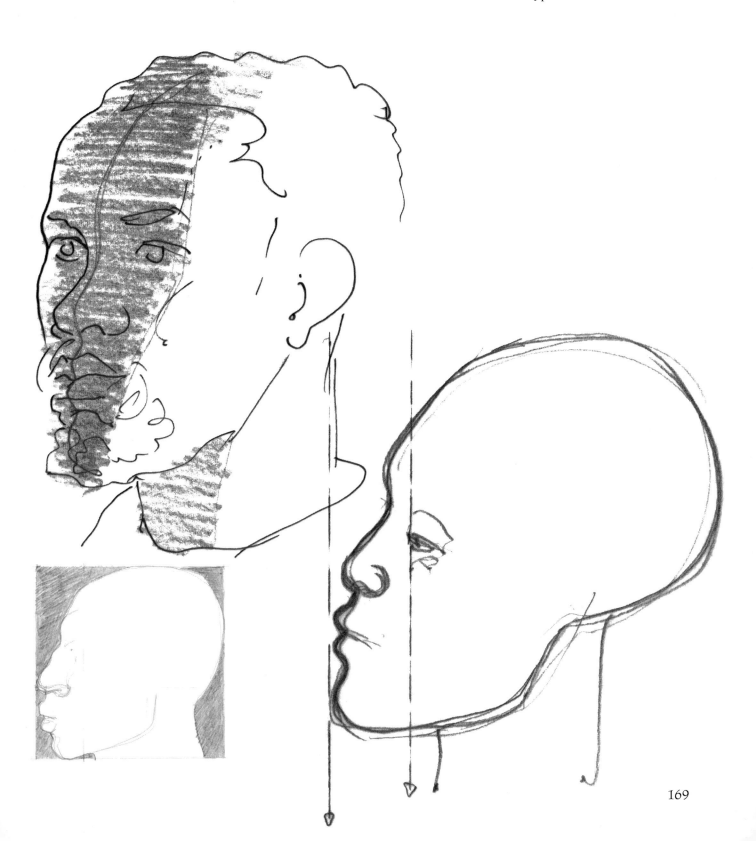

This European has a wide face caused by the large difference between the width of the cheek bones and the width of the skull. Ask yourself questions: for example, are the eyes unusually close together? Is the skull unusually wide?

An Oriental head is generally characterised by full cheek bones. This will influence the shape of the eye.

Be careful not to exaggerate the differences or the portrait will become a caricature.

Beards

The main point to remember is to draw the complete shape and then block in the general tone. Whenever possible, see how the beard follows the forms of the jaw, chin and upper lip.

Spectacles

Light falling directly on the front of the face of a person wearing spectacles will be reflected in the glass, making it difficult to see the shape of the eyes. Have the light coming from the side or from behind the head. You can use the shape of the spectacles to help you see the form of the head.

Group portraits

Make separate studies of each member of the group (pose, light, shape of head and shoulders), then make tracings of each drawing. Shift these tracings around until you have arranged a satisfactory composition.

The drawing below shows three views of the same head. The composition was established as described above. Note the line curving through each mouth and continuing through to the two outside shoulders. There is a similar curve through the eyes. These two curved lines form the basis of the composition.

A portrait step by step

Remember to let your pencil describe what you have seen and understood.

1. Feel for the shapes of the light and dark areas.

2. Constantly re-establish proportions (e.g. the position of the eye nearest to you in relation to the width of the head). Let your pencil flow from shape to shape and from point to point. Follow and continue the directions of lines (e.g. from the eye towards the ear, from the ear to the jaw and, in this case, from neck to brooch).

3. Gradually build up the tones, continually checking shapes (e.g. the light area of the upper lip) and relative points on a horizontal and vertical line (e.g. eye to corner of mouth to line of neck).

4. Be careful not to overwork the drawing. A simple line drawn with understanding has more life than an overworked line that is only half-understood.

The finished drawing is shown on the next page.